TOP DOG

Training the Retriever for Waterfowl and Upland Hunting

Joseph Middleton

DUTTON

DUTTON
Published by Penguin Group (USA) Inc.
375 Hudson Street, New York, New York 10014, U.S.A.
Penguin Books Ltd, Registered Offices: 80 Strand, London WC2R 0RL, England
Penguin Books Australia Ltd, 250 Camberwell Road, Camberwell, Victoria 3124, Australia
Penguin Books Canada Ltd, 10 Alcorn Avenue, Toronto, Ontario, Canada M4V 3B2
Penguin Books (NZ) Ltd, Cnr Rosedale and Airborne Roads, Albany, Auckland 1310,
New Zealand

Published by Dutton, a member of Penguin Group (USA) Inc.

First printing, March 2004
10 9 8 7 6 5 4 3 2 1

ISBN: 0-525-94788-4

Printed in the United States of America

This book is printed on acid-free paper. ∞

TABLE OF CONTENTS

PART I
TEACHING THE BASICS
WITHOUT THE ELECTRONIC COLLAR

PART II
REINFORCING THE BASICS
WITH THE ELECTRONIC COLLAR

PART III
SCHOOL'S OUT: REAL-WORLD DRILLS

1

C H A P T E R

Introduction

Too often we amateur dog trainers settle for too little from our dog. We buy a pup with the best intentions of creating a world-class retriever, but before too long we settle on some basic training and the vague hope that our dog's natural instincts will guide it to greatness. We all know how often that happens.

By following training techniques used by professional trainers like Tony Hartnett (shown here with a handful of trainees) you, too, can produce a "top dog."

On the other hand, we watch field trials or hunting dog trials with envy. These dogs perform miraculously at tasks that it seems impossible to ingrain in our own retrievers. The professional trainers, we console ourselves, have infinite time and a bag of tricks and techniques we cannot possibly learn.

Nothing could be further from the truth. The goal of this book is to provide you with training techniques used on the world's finest retrievers. Following these techniques, you can produce what we call a "top dog"—a dog that lives up to his full potential by consistently obeying your commands and making the most difficult of retrieves. A dog that is a pleasure to be with in the duck blind or the home. A dog that can be hunted safely with other dogs and hunters because he obeys commands without fail. A dog that will give you hours of pleasure hunting waterfowl or upland birds or one that is capable of showing his stuff in competitive trials. A dog, in short, you're proud to own.

There is nothing esoteric or complicated about developing a top dog. To the contrary, it is simply a process of teaching four basic commands and then extending those commands through a variety of lessons and drills. This book shows you how to select a puppy if you don't already have one, and then it shows you how to teach the basic lessons during his early days in preschool and school.

Then the training takes on a new dimension through the use of the electronic collar to reinforce the basic lessons and refine your dog's retrieving techniques. The electronic training collar is in near universal use by topflight professional trainers. In the hands of the right person, it is a wonderful training tool. Used improperly, it can be a disaster. I'll show you how to use the collar the right way—to reinforce lessons that have already been learned through conventional techniques. There is no voodoo or magic to it. The electronic collar, used the right way, is a fine and straightforward device for reinforcing behavior. It is never used to punish or to teach the lesson the first time. And it is never (well, almost never) used when the dog is in the water.

With the proper use of the electronic collar, you have at your disposal all the techniques the best of professional trainers would use. What you must add is time, patience, and consistency. Sure, professionals have more experience than you or I, but by consistently applying the right lessons you'll benefit from their experience without having to spend years learning the lessons the hard way. Be persistent. Be consistent. The experience will come as you and your retriever form an inseparable team.

There is no room for shortcuts. You must teach the basics first, using the tried-and-true methods. Then you reinforce those basic lessons using the electronic collar.

The attitude you bring to each training session is important. If you are tense or agitated from a problem at work, try to leave those troubles behind before beginning your training session. Dogs are intelligent creatures with emotional antennae that can pick up your own mental state.

A dog's attention span is short. Keep your training sessions short. A short training session each day is all you need to produce the top dog you've always wanted in just a few months.

Avoid perfectionism. Your dog may be on his way to top dog status, but he will certainly be capable of mistakes...just like his master.

Treat your retriever the way you want your boss to treat you. Don't yell at him for something he did wrong; show him how to do it right and then reward him for the effort. You'll learn here how to apply "pressure" to get your dog doing the right thing, but the emphasis is always on the positive, always on success.

Realize that all dogs are different. Each dog will take to these lessons at his own pace. Exercise your best judgment on how long to train, how hard to push the dog, how much to demand at each stage.

You'll gain an even clearer understanding of the lessons taught in this book if you also purchase the *Top Dog* and *Top Dog II* videos. Additional insight can be gained from the *Water Dog*, *Game Dog*, and *Family Dog* videos.

This is the beginning of a long relationship between you and your dog—a relationship you will remember and tell others about the rest of your life. Be patient. Be consistent. Be fair. And most of all, have fun.

• • •

2
CHAPTER

Picking a Puppy

Years ago I read a dog-training book written by a professional trainer that contained a chapter entitled "Everything I Know About Picking A Puppy." The pages were blank. The author's point was clear, but while there is no definitive method for picking a puppy, you can increase your odds by looking at the parents and by checking Pup's reactions to a few simple tests.

The most effective way to select a pup is to evaluate the dog's parents, paying particular attention to the kind of retrieving work the parents do. If the parents are field-trial champions, be aware that you're probably going to get a dog with enormous energy and desire. That may be more dog than you want or need. Avoid dogs with show pedigrees; show dogs are bred purely for confirmation and may have minimal hunting instincts. If you want a combination hunting dog and family dog with a calm disposition, look for parents that have those qualities.

The dog you select is likely to be with you for a good part of your hunting life. You'll devote countless hours to training the dog, hunting with him, and—just as important—living with him throughout the year. Besides time, you will commit an important part of yourself emotionally to your hunting companion. If you have a family, they will become deeply involved, as well.

The best way to evaluate the parents of a prospective pup, if you are able, is to watch the parents work in the field. Talk with the breeder about the line of dogs he breeds, and if the breeder employs a trainer for his or her own dogs, talk with that person also. Interview clients who have bought dogs from a previous breeding of the same parents or of similar bloodlines.

Finding breeders that produce the kind of retriever you are looking for may require a bit a detective work, but the effort will pay off. If you have a friend who is an avid duck hunter, ask who he recommends. Call members of your local Ducks Unlimited chapter to see what dogs they have bought and what bloodlines they recommend. Ask if you can see their dogs work in the field. If possible, hunt with the sire or dam. Volunteering to help with their training regimen is a good way to repay the favor and will teach you even more about the training process.

If you don't know someone who can personally recommend a kennel, you can look to organizations like the American Kennel Club (AKC), the Hunting Retriever Club (HRC), the North American Hunting Retriever Association (NAHRA), or the North American Versatile Hunting Dog Association (NAVHDA). Most such organizations have retriever hunt tests that effectively and honestly score a retriever's ability. If you get a pup from proven parents, you won't always hit the bull's-eye, but you will always, at the very least, hit the target. Once you find parents that are like the dog you want, there are other things to consider.

What size dog do you want? Are you keeping the dog in the house? There are some pretty big Labs out there. Again, the size of the parents is your best guide to the size the pups will be. Pay careful attention to the possibility of genetic defects. A very real problem among some retriever breeds is hip dysplasia. Never buy a pup unless it comes with certified records that show the bloodlines are free of hip dysplasia. Review these records with your small-animal veterinarian before buying a pup. One of the great (and expensive) heartbreaks is to have your dog bond with the family and make enormous progress in his training only to discover, around age two, that the dog is crippled with hip dysplasia. Demand certified records.

When you find a litter from proven parents that have the qualities you want in a hunting companion, it's time to pick the pup. There are a few tests you can use that may help you select the right pup. None are guaranteed, but they should point you in the right direction. The goal here is to eliminate the extremes—pups that are either overly aggressive or too passive. These test are based on a puppy behavior test developed by William E. Campbell and modified for the Labrador or golden retriever buyer by Richard A. Wolters in his *Water Dog* and *Game Dog* books.

Get all the pups in a safe, confined place in the yard. In order for these tests to have value, the puppies should be at least six weeks old and, of course, not older than forty-nine days—the age at which you should take your pup home. Make sure the grass is short enough for the pudgy little critters to get around easily. Watch them and see how they play. A playful pup is fine, but stay away from the one that seems to be overly aggressive with the other pups. You don't want the bully; he might grow up to be a fighter who's hard to keep around other dogs. You want a spirited hunting dog, not a delinquent.

Let the pups run around, and observe each one.

Likewise, avoid the wallflower. To take the training, a dog has to be bold—with a strong sense of self-confidence. The wallflower may grow out of that timid spirit, but why take the chance? Your best bet is a playful pup with an even disposition.

Look also for a pup that shows an interest in people. Take each pup away from his littermates and other distractions—again, to an area with short grass. Give him a chance to get acclimated to the new area. Make sure he's wide-awake. Toss a small wadded-up sock and watch how he chases it. Is he eager to chase? Does he want to get it in his mouth? If the puppy goes after it, he is demonstrating attention to an

Toss a wadded sock to test Pup's retrieving desire.

object. Retrieving the wadded sock demonstrates concentration and a desire to please.

Move a few feet away. Make sure Pup sees you, then kneel down, clap your hands, and call "pup, pup, pup" in a playful manner. If he runs to you, that's great. If he runs away or just sits there, give him another chance.

Pet the puppy from head to tail for thirty seconds. If he mouths and licks your hands while you're petting, that's a sign of a happy, confident pup that likes people. If he bites your hand (more than just mouthing it), growls, or slinks away in an effort to avoid your company, you should be concerned. Any puppy can have a bad moment. Give him another chance. But if this behavior repeats itself, this is probably not your dog. If the pup passes this test, move on to the restraint test.

To put the puppy through the restraint test, gently roll him over onto his back. Hold him there with your hand over his stomach and the area between his two front legs. It is a good sign if he struggles a

Roll Pup on his back and gauge his reaction.

Barring distractions, Pup should be eager to follow you around.

bit, then settles. This shows he is willing to happily defer to you as the boss. If he struggles fiercely the whole time you are holding him or if he just lies there passively, it is a good sign the puppy is either too aggressive or overly submissive.

Next, see if the little guy wants to go hunting with you. With no distractions around, walk past him, within a foot or two. Does he happily follow you? If so, that's a good sign. If he does not go with you, walk past him again and make sure he sees you. After several attempts, if he shows no interest at all (and there are no other distractions around that are a lot more interesting than you), then you've identified a characteristic that should at least raise some suspicion.

Let's see how your future dog reacts to a little discomfort. Take one of the puppy's front feet and gently pinch the area between the toes. A dog is sensitive to pressure in that area. Make the pinch reasonable. Don't overdo it. Gradually increase the pinch until you

The pinch test will tell you a lot about a pup's nature.

get a reaction. Take it as a good sign if the puppy feels the pinch, lets out a little yelp, and forgives you with an eager lick and tail wag. You should be concerned if the puppy overreacts to the pinch and is unforgiving. Likewise, watch for a pup that does not react to the pinch at all. That dog may have a high tolerance for pain and may need more forceful training later.

•   •   •

3
CHAPTER

Preschool Education

It wasn't that long ago that there was a belief among trainers that you shouldn't begin training setters for hunting until they were three years old. You could start a pointer, the conventional wisdom went, at age two.

Today it's hard to imagine anything quite so ridiculous. After all, these dogs' ancestors survived by hunting, and they learned to hunt well before two years of age or they starved.

The idea to begin training at age two or three may have originated when some people "trained" dogs by half beating them to death, or "breaking" them. A dog trained using that method had to be mature and self-confident to take the pain and stress of training. With the modern training methods, which include the proper use of the electronic collar, there is no need for significant pain in training—and certainly no need for whipping a dog or physically punishing him.

Dogs, like humans, are eager to learn from a very early age. Their survival depends on it. The key to good learning is to match the lessons to the animal's mental and physical readiness to learn. You want to provide early training opportunities when the dog is at the right stage—when he's eager and able to learn the lessons you present. In this regard, modern training has benefited greatly from the work on animal behavior done by Dr. J. Paul Scott and later by Dr. Michael Fox—work that was effectively introduced to the attention of the hunting community through Richard A. Wolters's *Water Dog* and *Game Dog* books.

Dr. Scott, director of the prestigious Animal Behavior Laboratory at Hamilton Station of the Roscoe B. Jackson Memorial Laboratory in Maine, directed a project to help the training program of Guide Dogs for the Blind, Inc. That worthwhile organization, following conventional wisdom, had always waited until the dogs were physically large enough to lead the blind before beginning the training. Dr. Scott's research, however, turned that around. His study showed that there are five periods during which a dog's ability to learn are at their peak. His research identified these periods as follows:

Days 0 to 21: Dr. Scott's research showed that puppies of all breeds have virtually no capacity for learning until they are twenty-one days old. During the first three weeks, however, a puppy does process simple information related to survival—reacting only to needs for warmth, food, sleep, and his mother.

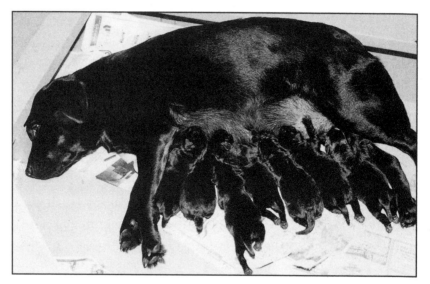

During the earliest stage of their lives, puppies rely solely on instinctive behaviors like feeding and nuzzling close to their mother.

Days 21 to 28: A puppy still has an absolute need for his mother during this period, but his eyes are opening and his senses are functioning now. These heightened senses open a new world that at times can be a bit forbidding and create emotional and social stress. A puppy's mother is of paramount importance.

Days 28 to 49: The puppy's world is beginning to open up. During this critical period, he will begin to recognize people and respond to

At exactly 49 days, Pup is ready to leave the nest and come home with you.

familiar voices. The pecking order, or social order of the litter, is beginning to form. The alpha dog takes his place. The wallflower begins to accept that position in the pecking order. The early stages of competition within the litter begin to form. The puppy also begins to learn a critical socializing skill during this stage—how to get along with other dogs. On the forty-ninth day exactly, Dr. Scott found, it's time to take Pup home. It's time for Pup to establish the most important bond of his life—the relationship he establishes with you. Now is the time for you to take the place of Pup's mother. Taking a puppy earlier could damage the bond with the mother and the socialization process with the littermates. Waiting longer would make it more difficult for the dog to establish a bond with humans.

Days 49 to 84: We call this period preschool. Pup is a sponge for learning. There is one trick, though. During preschool all the learning is done as play. There is no pressure to learn. None. No punishment. No pressure. All play. Pup is receiving valuable preschool training on important lessons like "sit," "here," and "fetch," but Pup doesn't even know it's learning; it's all fun and games.

Days 84 to 112: It's time for Pup to graduate to real schooling. From twelve weeks to sixteen weeks the bonding and the lessons continue, but now you can apply a little more pressure. The basics like "sit," "here," "heel," and "fetch" can now be taken more seriously. Pup learns disciplined behavior.

In early training, Pup may be learning important things like "sit," but to him it's all fun and games.

Communication

Watch any topflight trainer or hunter with his dog and you will, of course, see a dog with an enormous desire to find birds. But in the best man-dog teams you also find a deep sense of trust and communication, and chances are that bond was formed during the early weeks and months of the dog's life.

The French pride themselves on speaking the French language properly, with every nuance spoken to perfection. An American can move to France and learn the language at, say, age twenty, but no matter how well the American speaks the language, the French can tell the difference. Scientists have recently determined that a human being will never be able to speak a language perfectly, with all its nuances, unless that person has absorbed those subtleties by the age of three. After that age, the brain has developed to the point that it can't note and duly record those nuances.

For you and your dog to speak the same language you need to begin early—on the forty-ninth day. And words, or commands, are only one of the many ways you will communicate with Pup.

Say "kennel" as you tempt Pup into the crate with a piece of food. Reward him with the food and with praise and petting when he enters the crate.

Playing and Bonding

Keep your dog in the house if possible, at least during his early days with you. A dog that lives inside has far more opportunities to bond with you. He's with you while you are watching television, interacting with the family, preparing meals, or just relaxing. This gives the dog more time to observe you, your activities, and your voice.

It is equally important, however, to let Pup sleep in his own kennel box or crate. Some humans think it's cruel to make the animal sleep in a small confined space, but dogs feel safer and more in control when they have their own sleeping quarters. The crate is also an opportunity for Pup to learn one of his first commands—"kennel."

Cut a hot dog into bite-sized pieces. Open the door of the crate and toss one of Pup's favorite toys in. Get Pup's attention. Hold the food treat inside the crate and with great enthusiasm say "kennel." If Pup goes into the crate, reward him with praise and give him a piece of the hot dog. If Pup does not go into the crate, let him smell the food treat and then hold the treat inside the crate. Again, energetically say "kennel." At this point Pup should go into the kennel to get the treat. As he does, repeat the command "kennel" and reward him with the treat, praise him, and give him an affirming pet. After a while Pup should get the idea that if he goes into the crate when hearing the word "kennel," he will win this wonderful reward. I'll discuss food treats more later, but for now be assured that they work, especially during preschool.

No Gibberish

When you give a dog a command, even during the early stages when he is just beginning to associate a word with a behavior, simply give one clear command and then let it be. Do not add gibberish. Using the example of the "kennel" command, you should simply command "kennel." Do not say, "Comeonbaby. Comeonbaby. KennelforMama. GetinthisexpensivekennelIjustbought—now." To the dog, that's all distracting nonsense. You are trying to associate a behavior with a word. Make that word clear and simple.

Put yourself in the dog's position. Imagine you've suddenly landed in a world where you don't comprehend the language and the people there don't understand your language. You are placed in a room. You don't know why you are there. You wait. Finally a man comes into the room, approaches you, looks you in the eye, and says "goyo." You have no idea what he wants. You stand there. The man seems to be a little frustrated at your inability to understand, so once again he repeats "goyo." You don't know what to do. Clearly irritated, the man repeats "goyo." But you still do nothing. Finally, red-faced and raving, he shouts "goyo! goyo! X@$#*?!!!" You shrink, scared. This man wants something, but you don't know what. Finally, the fuming man stomps out of the room.

You wait, growing more anxious about not being able to figure out what this person wants. Soon, a kinder, gentler (and a lot smarter) man enters the room. He smiles and offers his hand. You take it and shake. Soon you begin to trust this person. This man takes your hand. You let him have it because you're not afraid of him. He places your hand on top of your head, smiles, and says "goyo." He lets go of your hand. Your hand drops to your side. The man takes your hand and, once again, places it on top of your head. As soon as your hand touches the top of your head, the man repeats one clear word: "goyo." The man lets go, and your hand, once again, drops to your side.

This time the man steps back, smiles, looks you in the eye in an affirming manner, and says "goyo." You're not sure, but you think that means put your hand on top of your head. Haltingly, you do that. The moment your hand hits the top of your head, the man smiles, nods, pats you on the back, and gives you a hundred-dollar bill.

Once again, with your hands at your side, the man looks you in the eye and says "goyo." This time, you can't get your hand to your head fast enough. When you do, he affirms that behavior with a smile and another reward of a hundred-dollar bill.

The point of this silly example is that you must let the dog know what behavior you want, and you have to associate that behavior with a word that will always be clear to the dog.

The foundation of a well-trained dog is a clear understanding of the basics of "here," "sit," "heel," and "fetch." Those basic behaviors must be associated with your command, either by voice or whistle. The sound that is associated with the behavior begins in preschool. It's all play for now, but you still want one clear, consistent voice command— no gibberish, please!

Food Rewards

You're about to weave early lessons of the basics into the fun of preschool, but first let's talk about the food treat as a reward.

I realize that a lot of you may be squirming uncomfortably at this moment because you have heard over the years that food treats should not be used to train a sporting dog. I've heard that, too. I never knew why. I have a friend who is adamant about not using food treats.

When you take Pup outside, and he is in the act of relieving himself, associate that behavior with a word like "potty." If you take Pup outside and he is not going "potty" on his own, this word will often encourage him to hurry up and get on with his business. Whatever word you use, be consistent. It should take about three to four weeks to housebreak your young dog. Be patient. Once he's trained, you've overcome a major hurdle.

Playing with the Basics

The basis of a well-trained dog—as I'll stress again and again—is a strong understanding of the basic commands of "here," "sit," "heel," and "fetch." You don't want to put any pressure on Pup to learn these commands until he is older. But since Pup is a sponge for learning at this early age, you'll begin to use play to associate the sound of a word with a behavior.

When rewarding Pup for a job well done, hold him gently by the collar while stroking and praising him.

To associate a word with a behavior, you must use the same word every time. It doesn't matter what the word is, as long as you use it consistently for the same behavior. For example, you can use either "here" or "come" to command the dog to come to you. Whichever you use is fine, but pick one word for the command and stay with it. Don't mix in alternative words. You're teaching the dog to associate a word with a behavior, not to speak English. Give one clear, consistent command.

Speak in a normal tone when praising Pup, no matter how ecstatic you might be that he performed as commanded. Shouting your happiness might scare Pup and make him associate something negative with what he has done. An exuberant, upbeat sound to your voice is fine as long as it's not a scream that scares him. Let Pup know you're happy. The tone of your voice is extremely important in dog training.

When giving Pup a treat, hold him by the collar and praise him. Praise him again after you give him the treat and stroke his shoulder.

When Pup successfully completes a task, hold him gently by the collar and stroke his shoulder, back, or head. Don't pat or "beat" Pup on the back or head. Hold the collar with one hand while gently stroking with the other and reassuring him with a calm, gentle voice.

If you're giving a food treat, hold pup's collar, praise him, give the food treat, and then praise again and stroke his shoulder. Hold Pup gently by the collar for a few seconds, then release him with a happy and upbeat "OK" command.

Even though he's a puppy, you still want to use clear, distinct commands. You don't really expect the puppy to fully understand the words, but you're planting the seeds for a strong understanding of simple, one-word commands. During preschool, never expect Pup to obey a command, and never punish him if he doesn't. In preschool everything is fun and games.

Introduce Pup to the leash by attaching it to his collar and letting him drag it around the yard.

Introducing the Leash

Before you begin to associate words with behaviors, you must introduce your new puppy to the leash, or check cord. (The word leash usually means a short lead used for handling a dog at close range, and a check cord refers to a longer lead used in field training exercises.) When you bring Pup home, he should have a lightweight collar that fits him properly. When Pup is acclimated to the home and the people in it, purchase a lightweight leash that clips to the collar. Clip the leash to Pup and let him drag it around the yard. This lets him get used to the leash without it becoming threatening. You need the leash because you need to be able to control Pup even during these early days of play training. You do not need to control Pup if you're just playing, but if you're trying to associate a word with a behavior, the leash can help you to make that connection.

When Pup is used to dragging his leash around, take him for a walk in a quiet, safe place. Avoid areas with loud cars, roaring motorcycles, and mean, barking dogs. Soon, he will begin to get the idea that this leash means control—his first gentle lesson that when he is with you, you are in charge of the situation.

Fun and Games

Recruit a training partner and go to a fenced-in area so Pup can't run away and get into the street. Your back yard is perfect if it's fenced. If not, a fenced-in little league baseball field can be an excellent area to work your dog.

While your partner holds Pup on the leash, play with Pup and get excited so that he'll want to chase you. When Pup is raring to go and you're sure he's watching you, say Pup's name, then run away. As your partner releases the leash, Pup will think it's great fun to chase and find you. When he is running toward you, drop to a knee, say his name, and add the word "here" or the word "come," whichever you choose to use as your permanent command.

When Pup reaches you, praise him, give him a food treat, pet him, praise him again, hold him in place for a couple of seconds, and then release him with an upbeat "OK." The pup has no earthly idea that you're teaching him the early lessons for "here." He just knows this is fun. Little by little, Pup begins to associate the behavior of coming to you with the sound of the word "here" or "come."

You are simply trying to associate a word with a behavior. Do not say the word "here" or "come" unless you're sure Pup is running to you. You don't want to associate a word with a behavior unless you are certain he is carrying out the correct behavior. And certainly don't reprimand him if things don't go as planned.

This game can be played in your house and you can run away from Pup and hide inside closets and behind chairs. This will get him even more interested and excited.

You can also perform a variation of this game without an assistant. Run out ahead of Pup, turn, and drop to a knee. When you're sure he's running to you, say his name, followed by "here" (from this point on I'll refer to this command as "here" although you may choose to use "come"). If Pup runs right to you, praise him and give him a treat.

It's also a good idea to praise Pup and give him a treat anytime he runs to you on his own. This conditions the "here" response without the verbal command. It reminds Pup that coming to you is fun and rewarding.

Another great way to use the food treat at this early stage is with name recognition. Say Pup's name, and if he turns his attention to you, reward him with a food treat.

Early Lessons in the "Sit" Command

"Sit" is a command you'll use every day in the life of your retriever. You can start "sit" during the preschool stage with play—never saying the word "sit."

When you're playing with Pup, hold a food treat over Pup's head. Hold it close enough that he can smell it. When Pup rocks back to smell the treat, his butt will hit the ground. The moment Pup's butt hits the ground—give Pup the food treat. Don't add the word "sit" at this preschool stage. If he sits, he gets the treat. He's going to associate sitting with a good thing!

Early Play for the "Fetch" Command

Attach a toy to a leash. Dangle the toy in front of Pup and play with him. The leash puts you in control of the toy. When Pup is excited, toss the toy out a few feet in front of Pup. See if he thinks it's fun to pick up the toy and bring it back to you.

A narrow hallway is the perfect place for Pup's early "fetch" training, as it gives him little room to run away with the object.

After a while, when you're sure Pup is going to run out and pick up the toy and bring it to you, add the command "fetch." If pup brings you the toy, when you used the word "fetch," praise him, and give him a food treat. Hold Pup a few seconds then release with a happy "OK."

Another fun way to play fetch is in the hallway of your home. Close the doors to the rooms along the hallway, so Pup won't make a detour. Using a plastic toy (or any other object that it's OK for Pup to retrieve — not a bedroom slipper), get down on a knee at one end of the hallway. Excite Pup with the object and toss it down the hallway. The puppy should bound away to get the object. When he is returning to you with the object, add the word "fetch." If Pup brings the object right to you, praise him and give him a treat. But it's OK even if he tries to sneak past you with the toy. As he tries to pass, give the command "fetch" as you pull Pup to you. When he gives you the toy, praise him and give a treat.

If you toss the toy and Pup does not go to get it, do not use the word "fetch." You only want to add the command when the behavior is being properly obeyed.

The "No" Command

Teaching Pup the meaning of "no" is a good lesson to begin in preschool. You want preschool to be fun and exciting, but there are also behaviors you want Pup to associate with the "no" command and the sound of a harsh voice. In dog training the tone of the voice can be extremely effective. At this stage, Pup can begin to learn the sound of your voice if you are displeased.

If Pup nips your hand in a painful way, cry like a pup and say "no" in a harsh voice. Don't pull your hand away quickly. Pup may think the moving hand is an exciting object to chase and nip. After you say "no" in a harsh voice, immediately put something in front of Pup that he is permitted to bite—like his toy. That gives you the opportunity to turn a harsh "no" into a positive win. You're saying, in essence, "You can't bite me, but you can bite this." The same idea holds for furniture. If you catch him chewing furniture say "no" in a harsh voice, then turn Pup's attention to a toy he is permitted to chew. Eventually he will know that a harsh "no" means that what he is doing is an unwanted behavior that he should stop immediately.

Never use the "no" command unless Pup is actually caught in the act. No puppy can understand that what he did twenty seconds ago is now a "no." You have to catch him in the act. That's part of your job as a trainer.

Preschool is also a great time to use Pup's name often. Give Pup a clear, easily understandable name soon after you bring him home. Use that name whenever you can.

According to Dr. Scott's research, preschool begins on the forty-ninth day of the dog's life. I can't guarantee that good preschool work will make your dog a top dog, but I can guarantee the puppy will be untrainable if you bring it home, put it in the kennel, give it no name, pay no attention to it, and a year or so later try to train it.

Bring your pup home on the forty-ninth day of his life and immediately enroll him in a fun and enjoyable preschool routine. Lay the foundation for the kind of communication, training, and relationship that will one day result in a top dog.

• • •

CHAPTER

School: Teaching the Basics with Voice and Whistle

In preschool you introduced the basics through fun and games, without pressure or correction. All fun and games. Now, though, Pup is getting a little older. At twelve weeks of age, it's time to teach the basics and add a little pressure, if necessary, to make sure Pup obeys the command. This period is called school.

A word of caution, however. Never apply pressure, even lightly, unless you're sure that Pup knows what you want him to do.

You begin the training process by associating a word with a behavior. The dog doesn't understand English, but eventually he will come to associate a word with a behavior. If you wanted to teach your dog to sit on the sound of "Elvis," you would say the word "Elvis," push pup's butt to the ground, and reward and praise the pup as soon as his butt hits the floor. It wouldn't be long before that pup would know that when he hears the word "Elvis," he will be praised and rewarded if he puts his butt on the ground.

There is no magic in the word, but there is magic in the consistency. If you're going to use the word "Elvis" for the sit command, you must use that same word every time. Repetition and consistency are fundamental to the basics. But let's not use the word "Elvis." No use in confusing your hunting partner. Instead, let's talk about how to associate the word "sit" with that behavior.

By now, Pup should be familiar with dragging the leash around the yard. Take Pup out to the training area on the leash. The training area should be fenced (for Pup's safety) and free of distractions like playing children and speeding cars. The training area should also be away from other dogs. There is no way a dog can concentrate on what you want with five other dogs yapping at him.

Teaching the "Sit" Voice Command

Walk along with Pup on the leash. Stop. Just as you stop, pull gently up on the leash while pushing Pup's butt gently, but firmly, to the ground. As soon as Pup's butt hits the ground say "sit" in a firm but upbeat voice. Don't blather on with other descriptions of the act of sitting. It's all gibberish to him. Just say "sit" as soon as Pup's butt hits the ground. Hold Pup there for two seconds so he has time to get it in his head that there's something special about that sit position. After that two seconds, praise Pup, pet him, and give him a food treat. When Pup has had a chance to eat his reward, say "OK" in a happy, upbeat voice and, holding the leash, walk

The "sit" command. Pull on the leash while pushing Pup's butt gently to the ground.

forward at a brisk pace. After you've walked a short way, repeat the exercise in exactly the same manner.

Again, when you praise Pup don't shout and squeal in delight; it might scare him. Speak in a calm, firm, upbeat voice when you praise Pup. Let him know you're happy in your tone, but don't be loud. Your tone of voice is often at least as important as the words.

Practice the "sit" command every day, if possible. If a training session every day seems too much for Pup, try every other day. There is no rule for how long the session should last, but keep the sessions short and if you feel that Pup seems "burned out"—his tail droops or the training sessions don't seem fun—then bring the session to a close. With repetition and consistency, you should begin to see results soon.

One of the best rewards for a retriever after a training session is throwing fun bumpers—a bumper, or training dummy, thrown and retrieved just for the joy of it. You throw it. The dog brings it to you. You throw it again. No rules. No pressure. Just fun. Fun bumpers are a reward for a job well done. After throwing fun bumpers for a short while, praise the dog and end the training session for the day.

"Sit" Also Means "Stay"

There is no actual command for "stay." When you teach Pup to "sit" that means sit until I give you another command. So "sit" means "stay."

With a little practice, Pup will remain in the sitting position even as you move farther and farther away.

When Pup is doing well on the "sit" command, put him into the sit position, then step slowly away. If Pup tries to follow you, pull up on the leash, command "sit," and, by applying pressure to Pup's rear, put him back into the sit position. Praise him for sitting, then slowly back away again. Start with five feet. If he remains seated, come back, praise and treat, and then move forward and do the exercise again. The next day, go to ten feet and so on. Eventually, through praise, reward, and repetition, Pup will get the idea that you want him to continue to sit until you come back and release him with an upbeat "OK." ("OK" is not a command. It's simply a word to let Pup know that that part of the lesson is over and you're moving to another lesson.)

The commands in the field that would allow a dog to leave the sit position are "here," "fetch," the dog's name, or the command "back," which you will later learn is the dog's signal to leave the sit position to make a blind retrieve.

Pup must have a solid understanding of "sit" before you begin to teach the other voice commands.

Teaching the "Here" Voice Command

The "here" (or "come") command means "Come here now." It does not mean come when you're ready. It means now.

You deliver the "here" command differently depending on whether the dog is moving or stationary. If he's moving, say the dog's name first, then give the "here" command. The name gets the dog's attention; the word "here" gives the command. If the dog is seated or stationary, meaning you already have his attention, then give the "here" command without first saying his name.

To teach the "here" command, put Pup on the check cord and place him in the sit position. Since he now knows that "sit" means "Sit and stay until I give you another command," you should be able to walk away from Pup while he continues to sit.

Move slowly away from Pup, continuing to command "sit." When you reach the end of the leash, drop down on one knee and command "here." Again, tone is important. Say "here" in an upbeat, happy tone that would be inviting to a dog. Again, add no gibberish. The pup should run to you eagerly. When Pup reaches you, praise and stroke him, then give him a food treat. After Pup has had a moment for all this to sink in, stand up and, with Pup still on the leash, repeat the exercise.

As Pup gets better and better, go to a longer leash or check cord. A lightweight nylon rope will allow you to lengthen the lesson with the same training tool.

When teaching the "here" command, always use a leash or check cord. You must always be able to enforce any command you give, or Pup will learn that he doesn't have to obey you.

If Pup does not obey the "here" command, give a light tug on the rope, pulling Pup to you, associating the sound with the behavior. When Pup reaches you, give praise and a treat even if you and the rope are the only reason the little devil finally got to you. If he has any sense at all, he will soon make the association that coming to you on the "here" command will bring him a paycheck.

During this stage of working with the "here" command, do not work without Pup on a check cord. If you put him in the sit position and give the "here" command, you have to be certain that you can enforce that command. If you don't have him on a cord and he runs off in the other direction on the "here" command, you're reinforcing Pup's understanding that he does not have to obey you. This is a dangerous road to travel. Never give a command you can't enforce.

A long hallway is a good place to work on "here." Close the doors along the hallway so there's no escape route. Put Pup in the sit position, then back slowly down the hallway, repeating the command "sit." When you command "here," Pup has nowhere to go but directly to you. It's a "win" situation, and he is praised and rewarded for it.

Teaching the "Heel" Voice Command

In training a bird dog, you can get by with a basic understanding of "whoa," "here," and "fetch." It's nice if a bird dog knows "heel," but it is not essential. A retriever, on the other hand, must understand "heel" and must eventually be able to obey the command instantly and every time.

A working retriever must be able to heel. When teaching this important command, be consistent. "Heel" should mean the same thing every time.

The behavior you want with the "heel" command is specific. "Heel" doesn't mean "Come somewhere nearby and stand behind me." It means that Pup must put his head alongside your right knee and face in the same direction you are facing. He needs to move into the proper position regardless of whether you are standing, walking, or even riding a bicycle, which some owners do when exercising their dog.

To teach the voice command for "heel" put Pup on the leash and go for a walk in your established training area. When he is out at the end of the check cord, either ahead of you or behind you, command "here" while continuing to walk. When his head comes alongside your knee, add the command "heel." Praise Pup and continue to walk. If he pulls away, snatch him back into position with the cord and the moment his head is back in the correct position repeat the command "heel."

The moving heel is important, but it's also extremely important for a retriever to be able to heel when the handler is standing still. To teach "heel" when you are standing still call Pup to you. As he approaches, command "heel," and use the leash to pull him around until he is facing the same direction you are facing and his head is next to your right knee. Once he is firmly in position, repeat the command "heel," hold him in that position for two seconds, praise him, give him a treat, and release him with an upbeat "OK." Continue the exercise until your common sense tells you it's enough for one day.

Some trainers combine a hand signal with the voice command to train a dog to step around into the heel position. Tony Hartnett puts it like this: "I want to give the dog every possible opportunity to obey the command. If a consistent hand signal helps him understand what I want, then I use it." With the dog out ahead of him, Tony commands "here." As the dog approaches, Tony

Giving a hand signal when commanding "heel" helps Pup move into the correct heel position.

holds his right arm outstretched toward the dog and sweeps it around to his right side, commanding "heel." The hand sweeping slowly to his side is a visual aid that helps the dog associate the command with the behavior that he wants.

Teaching the "Down" Voice Command

To teach the voice command for "down," put Pup in the sit position. Take his front legs and pull them gently to you. When his stomach reaches the ground command "down." Hold him in that position for two seconds, and then praise him and give a treat. After a few lessons, he will know exactly what you want.

Teaching the "Kennel" Voice Command

As mentioned in an earlier chapter, it seems to work best to keep Pup in the house. There are more opportunities for training and bonding. By now, Pup should be sleeping through the night in his crate. You should have already been associating the command "kennel" with Pup entering his crate and finding a food treat. The kennel, in Pup's opinion, should be a happy, safe place.

To teach this command at an older age, simply continue to do what you've already been doing. Lead Pup to the crate, open the door, and command "kennel." When he enters the kennel, praise him and give him a treat. If he does not enter the kennel, repeat the command and gently but forcibly push him into the crate. As soon as Pup is in the crate, stroke him, praise him with an upbeat, happy tone, and reward with a food treat.

Now that your dog is older, it's time to extend the kennel command to places like the car, the dog box on your truck, or an outside pen. Again, associating the behavior with the command is done in exactly the same way. When Pup is familiar with the box, open it, tap the inside of the box and command "kennel." If he jumps in, praise and treat. If he does not obey the command, pick him up, place him gently into the box, repeat the command, and then praise and treat. He'll get the idea soon, especially if that dog box is something that takes him on a ride that leads to the excitement of birds.

Use the same methods you used earlier to get Pup to "kennel" in a vehicle. Later, when he realizes that a car ride can lead to the excitement of retrieving birds, he'll be more than eager to jump right in.

Whistle Commands for the Basics

I won't repeat the training for whistle commands in the same detail I used for voice commands. Suffice it to say that the trainer does the same things, except, this time, the trainer associates a behavior with the sound of a whistle instead of the sound of the word. Other than that, the training is exactly the same.

"Sit" on the Whistle Command: As always, have Pup on the check cord. Walk him in your training area. Command "sit." He should sit on the voice command. Praise him, release with the upbeat "OK," then continue to walk. As you walk, blow one short blast on the whistle and pull up on his cord as you push his butt to the ground. The moment Pup's butt hits the ground, praise him and give him a food

The whistle "here" command. If Pup doesn't come right away, give a gentle tug on the check cord.

treat. Soon he will realize that if he sits the moment he hears one short blast on the whistle, he will receive praise and a food treat.

"Here" on the Whistle Command: The whistle command for "here" is a long, drawn-out whistle as if it is saying, "heeeer-rrrreeee." It is very important that the whistle command for "here" is clearly distinguishable from the short whistle command for "sit."

With Pup on the check cord, put him in the sit position. Step away from him. When you reach the end of the leash, turn to him and give the voice command "here." As he runs to you, give the long blast on the whistle. When Pup reaches you, praise and treat.

When you feel the time is right, try "here" with the whistle command alone. Put Pup in the sit position. Step away and, with the dog still on the cord, blow the whistle command for "here." If Pup comes to you, praise him and give him a treat. If he does not come to you, blow the whistle command and, as you do so, give a gentle tug on the cord. When Pup reaches you, praise and treat. Continue the exercise. Soon Pup will make the connection and will come running on the sound of the whistle command.

• • •

5
CHAPTER

Further Adventures in School

Conditioning to water and gunfire are not commands, but they are a part of preschool education because they are experiences that must be learned early through fun and games. If you go through all the work to train your dog but don't prepare him for the water or the sound of the gun, you're asking for trouble.

Conditioning Pup to Water

If your dog is a well-bred retriever, getting him to love water is going to be easy. But still, to paraphrase the old song, "break it to him gen-

A good retriever is born to love water; all you have to do is make sure he gets the proper introduction to it. Toss a bumper about two feet out into the water.

tly." The last thing you want to do is make Pup afraid of the water. Do you have a child? When you introduced your child to water, did you take her out and fling her into the nearest raging river? Of course, you didn't. Use the same common sense with your young retriever that you used with your child.

Walk Pup to water's edge. It should be a quiet, shallow pond. He should have been retrieving bumpers for fun and play since the day you brought him home. The bumper is nothing new to him. He knows what it is, and he wants to have the thrill of retrieving it. Now toss the bumper a few feet out into the shallow water. Give the "fetch" command in an upbeat, happy voice and see what Pup does. He may bound in after it.

If Pup doesn't go in after the bumper, wade into the water yourself and "jitterbug" the bumper in front of him to get his attention.

It's more likely, though, that Pup will be hesitant. He may study the water cautiously. That's fine; it shows he has good survival instincts. Toss the bumper into the shallow water again, giving that happy, upbeat "fetch" command. If Pup still seems unsure of the water, wade out into the water and "jitterbug" the bumper around in front of Pup to get his attention. When Pup shows excitement for the bumper,

Soon he'll bound right in after the bumper.

toss it just far enough into the water that he will have to get his feet wet to get it. As soon as Pup gets the bumper, praise him and try it again. This time, get Pup to go a little farther out into the water. A few of these exercises might be enough for the first day.

The next day, try tossing the bumper from the bank. Pup should be familiar with the water by now and will probably bound after the bumper with great enthusiasm. If he doesn't, wade back into the water and excite him with the "jitterbug bumper." He'll soon come in after it.

After Pup is wading into the water to retrieve the bumper, the next step is to increase the distance. Simply toss the bumper out farther, giving an upbeat command of "fetch." Your dog will soon be swimming out, retrieving bumpers, and returning them to you.

You started in a shallow part of the pond, so Pup could wade into the water. The next step is to get him to dive into the water. To give him the experience of diving, go to a part of the pond where it's deeper off the bank. Toss the bumper and give the "fetch" command. If Pup is feeling comfortable in the water, he will probably dive in after it.

This is also a good time to introduce Pup to the boat. Put him into a boat, using the already familiar "kennel" command. Position the boat in shallow water so that when Pup first jumps out of the boat, he

In the course of your training, Pup will learn that he has permission to leave the sit position on the command "back" in order to look for a blind. The command "back" is his signal that he will be following your guidance to find the downed bird. If, on the other hand, Pup was able to mark the downed bird, the command to send him on the marked retrieve will be his name, not the command "mark." "Mark" is a word used in training which means "Heads up. Get ready. Something is about to happen."

Staying in "Sit"
Until Hearing Another Command

So far, you've been throwing the bumper and giving the "fetch" command. The pup has been running for that bumper as soon as it's thrown. Now, you want to teach Pup to sit and not leave that position until he receives permission.

To teach Pup to be steady, toss a bumper and restrain Pup with the leash and command "sit" when he attempts to go after it.

Put Pup on a leash, walk him around your training area, and give the "sit" command. While continuing to hold the leash, toss the bumper out in front of Pup. Don't say anything. Most likely he will go after the bumper. Stop Pup with the leash and give the "sit" command. He should sit right away. Toss the bumper again and don't say anything. If Pup goes after the bumper, pull him back with the leash and give him the "sit" command once again. No gibberish, just pull him back and give the command. If he is crazy to get that bumper, pull up on the leash and push down on his rear to force him into the sit position. Then, as always, praise him for doing what you asked.

Toss the bumper again. By now Pup may be getting the message that he needs to stay seated. When it's clear that he is waiting in the sit position, say his name in a clear, upbeat manner—using the same tone you used to command "fetch." At this point, it's the tone of voice you're using when speaking Pup's name instead of "fetch" that should encourage him to get up and run for the bumper. When he gets back with the bumper, praise him and give him a treat.

Over time Pup will make the connection that he is praised and rewarded if he sits until hearing the sound of his name. He will not forget the word "fetch." He just learns that his name is also a sound that makes it OK to leave the sit position to make a retrieve.

When Pup is holding steady in the training area, take him to the field. You'll need a helper. With your dog on a twenty-five-foot check cord, put him in the sit position next to you. When you're sure he is watching—so this retrieve is sure to be a mark—have your helper throw a bumper in front of the dog. Pup should remain in the sit position. When it's clear that he is waiting for permission to leave that position, release Pup to retrieve the bumper by using his name. If Pup is not steady—that is, able to remain in the sit position while the bumper is thrown—put him back in the sit position and repeat the process until he is steady. It may take several sessions for this to happen, so be patient.

Once you're confident that Pup is steady in the field, bring him to the water for some further refinement. Put him in the sit position at water's edge. Have your helper in a boat throw a bumper into the water. When you feel that Pup is holding steady and waiting for the command, release him with the sound of his name.

It is important to have a dog that is steady, but you don't want to teach this lesson prematurely. Before forcing a dog to be steady, you should make sure he thinks retrieving a bumper is the most fun thing in the world. The dog should love to retrieve and feel happy and confident about retrieving. Trying to steady a young dog too soon can take away his desire to retrieve.

Another thing to keep in mind is the dog's name. From this point on, every time your dog leaves to retrieve a mark, he will leave on the sound of his name. With that in mind, a name like "Skip" will prove a lot easier to repeat than, say, "Witherspoon." And don't give your dog a name that he might confuse later with the sound of "back," the critical command used to retrieve blinds.

The Training Crop

So far I've talked about rewarding correct behavior, but I have not talked about punishment for incorrect behavior. But now that your puppy is between thirteen and sixteen weeks and receiving lessons that may need correction, you can apply some mild punishment if necessary. When you're sure Pup is old enough to take it, you can sting him slightly using a riding crop, or training crop—the kind used by horse trainers.

Timing is critical. If you sting the dog at the right moment, he'll make the connection with his behavior at that moment and with your

The training crop should only be used as a mild form of punishment. When Pup is disobedient, give him a slight sting with the crop and command "no."

harsh voice delivering a reprimand. If your timing is not right, you can beat on the dog all day and produce nothing but a confused and resentful animal. Under no circumstances should you use the training crop to deliver anything more than a mild sting. Do not use it to punish the animal or vent your frustration. If you are angry, gather up your training aids, go home, and save training for a day when you are calm and collected.

Let's say that you put your dog in the sit position in the field. Your helper throws a bumper. You have not given a command, but Pup leaves to make the retrieve anyway. Using the check cord to immediately pull him back into the sit position, try again. If after a few more attempts Pup still does not seem to be making the connection, you can give him a sting with the training crop to reinforce the point.

Put him in the sit position again and have your helper throw the bumper. Say nothing. If Pup leaves to make the retrieve without the command, immediately tell him "no" in a sharp tone and put him in the sit position. Repeat "no," sting him lightly with the training crop, and say "no" again. Pup should remain seated. Let him sit and think about it for a while, then try again.

Sooner or later, through a combination of positive behavior reinforcement and a little sting accompanied by an unhappy tone of voice, your dog will come to understand that he needs to stay seated until he hears the sound of his name.

Honoring Another Dog

There is one more basic—honoring—I need to teach before we move on to more advanced training. When a pointing breed backs, or "honors," another dog it means that he stops and points on seeing another dog already on point; he honors the dog that has already found the birds.

With a retriever, the word "honor" means that a dog should stay in the sit position and honor another dog that has been given permission to make the retrieve.

For example, let's imagine that two hunters are in a blind and each has his own retriever. A duck passes over and one hunter knocks it down. If the retrieve was a mark, both dogs are by now eyeing that downed bird, quivering in anticipation of making the retrieve. Etiquette dictates that the hunter who shot the duck has the privilege of sending his dog. To do that, he would simply say his dog's name and the dog would leave the sit position to make the retrieve. The second dog should remain in the sit position and honor the dog that is asked to make the retrieve.

You can only teach your dog to honor after he is well versed in the "sit" command. Pup must be secure in knowing that he does not have permission to leave the sit position until he is released by the sound of his name or another command. If he will not consistently obey that command alone in your training area, he certainly will not be able to do it with another dog making a retrieve in front of him.

Once Pup knows with certainty that he can't leave the sit position until he hears his name, put him with another retriever that is already well trained in his ability to honor. Let's say, for example, that the well-trained dog is named Tom. The dog you are training is Rocky. With your dog on a check cord, put both dogs in the sit position. Show them a bumper and say "mark." Remember, "mark" is not a command. It simply means "Heads up. Something is about to happen."

Toss the bumper in front of both dogs. Give them a moment to drool over the possibility of making the retrieve, then say, "Tom," the name of the already-trained dog. Tom will make the retrieve. Your dog, Rocky, should stay seated.

If Rocky has other ideas, command "no," and stop him with the check cord. Put Rocky back into the sit position, repeat "no" in an angry tone, and sting him with the crop. Repeat "no." If your timing is right, Rocky will know that you're unhappy with what he did.

The reason you could use the training crop on Rocky was because he already knew what to do, but the thought of making that retrieve made him so excited that he decided to ignore the sit-and-stay-until-further-orders position. It's your job to remind him.

Put both dogs back in the sit position. Say "mark" and toss the bumper ahead of them. Wait a beat, then say, "Tom." Tom will leave to make the retrieve. If Rocky goes too, bring him back with the check cord, put him back into the sit position, and repeat the process. It may

To teach honoring, have Pup sit while a fully trained dog makes the retrieve. If Pup moves, command "no" and stop him with the leash.

take two or three days, but soon Rocky will get it through his head that the only behavior you will praise and reward is when he honors Tom.

When Rocky gets this lesson through his head, reward him by letting him make the retrieve. This is one reason you must teach the lesson with a well-trained bracemate. If Tom does not obey the command when it's Rocky's turn, he will set Rocky back in the training.

There are two variations on these training methods for honoring. Let's say that Tom is given permission to make the retrieve. Tom leaves to make the retrieve, and as soon as he does, Rocky tries to make the retrieve, too. If you give the "sit" command by voice or whistle to correct Rocky, that command may confuse Tom and cause him to sit, as well.

One way around this problem is to spread the dogs out by some thirty feet. Have one handler next to Rocky and another handler next to Tom. Toss the bumper, then give Tom permission to make the retrieve. If Rocky tries to go, give the "sit" command so that it's loud enough for Rocky to hear but not loud enough to confuse Tom.

Another way to stop Rocky is to let him stop himself. To do that, you'll need a check cord at least ten feet long. With both dogs in the heel position, toss a bumper and release Tom on the sound of his name. If Rocky breaks to make the retrieve, don't say a thing; just hold onto that check cord (and make sure you have gloves on). When Rocky hits the end of the check cord, he will come to an abrupt stop all on his own. A few times of that, and he'll get the idea that it's not his turn.

When Rocky begins to wait his turn, go back to the line and bring both dogs into the heel position. Throw the bumper and give Tom permission to make the retrieve. If Rocky so much as raises his butt two inches off the ground, crop him and command "sit." At this point Tom should be far ahead, making the retrieve, and your quiet command to Rocky should not confuse Tom.

Soon enough, Rocky will get the idea that he does not have permission to make the retrieve until he hears the sound of his name. When he gets this in his head, by all means let him make the retrieve. The greatest reward for any retriever is making the retrieve. Soon he will come to realize that, if he is patient and honors the other dog, eventually he will have his reward.

It's time to move on from the basics, but in truth you will never leave the basics behind. No matter how good Pup gets, you will continuously be reminding him of the few lessons that form the foundation for any well-trained retriever. Ninety percent of the rest of the training you give Pup is about reinforcing those basics.

•   •   •

6
CHAPTER

The Force Retrieve

There will be days in your hunting career with Pup when the air is frigid, the water is almost ice, and there's a stiff north wind blowing just to keep things interesting. Those are the days that many ordinary retrievers have second thoughts about diving into the water to make a retrieve. But in developing a top dog, you want a retriever that will go into the water every time you give the command to retrieve.

Even though your dog may already love to retrieve, the force retrieve method—also referred to as the conditioned retrieve, force-fetching, and force-breaking—will give you the control you need to teach Pup to retrieve every time.

The force-retrieve training does just what the name implies: It forces the dog to make a retrieve. Done properly, it's not inhumane or especially difficult, but it does put pressure on the dog. So it's important that you not begin the force retrieve until you know your dog is mature enough emotionally to take the pressure. You also must make certain that your dog has all of his adult teeth before teaching the force retrieve. If the dog has tender gums from teething, the force retrieve will be painful to the dog's gums. You do not want to associate pain with the act of retrieving.

To teach the force retrieve, you want to get Pup up off the ground and onto a force fetch table, like the one shown on the next page. A dog feels in control on the ground, where his instincts tell him that he can escape the pressure. You want to take away the feeling that he can escape. Putting the dog on the force-fetch table puts you in control. Remember the rule: Never give a dog a command that you can't enforce. The leash gave you the power to enforce commands on the ground. The table gives you the power to enforce the force retrieve off the ground.

Long and narrow, the force-fetch table inhibits Pup from trying to get away and lets you control the training.

Ideally, the force-fetch table should be two feet wide. If you don't want to build a table, though, a long picnic table will work. Using any method you can devise, run a small cable about the size of a clothesline down the center of the force-fetch table. The cable should be three to four feet above the table, depending on the height of your dog. If you want to get fancy, a narrow pipe is even more stable than a cable. Connect a pulley to the cable (or pipe) and tie a short rope or chain (a tether) to the pulley. Attach a clip to the opposite end of the tether, as seen in the photograph. The

Rig a pulley and chain to a cable suspended three feet above the table, as shown.

tether is designed to hang from the pulley and attach to your dog's collar. The cable, pulley, and tether should be designed so that your dog is able to walk from one end of the table to the other, but the tether should be short enough so that he cannot jump off the table.

Warning: Never leave a dog alone when tethered to a force-fetch table. If he did manage to get off the table, he might not be able to get back on and could strangle himself before you return.

Once you've got Pup up on the table, do your best to make him feel comfortable. This is a new experience, and new experiences create anxiety in dogs and humans. For the first couple of days just put Pup on the table. Pat him, praise him, and make him feel at ease. If he cries and pulls at the tether, pet him to let him know it's OK. When he's comfortable with the table, leave him alone on it while you sit under a tree nearby and watch him. When you are sure your dog is comfortable on the table, it's time to take the first step in teaching the force retrieve.

For this lesson, you'll need a tool called a dowel. You can buy them from training supply stores or you can make one from a seven-inch piece of a wooden broom handle or similar round stock. Attach wooden squares to each end of the dowel so it looks like a small wooden dumbbell. The square ends make it easier for Pup to get his mouth under the dowel when he picks it up from the table.

The wooden dowel should have a square on each end to allow Pup to get his mouth around it and pick it up from the table.

With Pup on the table tethered to the cable, put him in the sit position. By now, he should obey it immediately. Shorten Pup's tether, as shown, to give you more control during this part of the exercise. If Pup is able to pull his head away or lower his head to try to run, you will only make the training session more difficult for both of you.

Shorten the tether so Pup can't duck or pull away.

Use your thumb and forefinger to force Pup to open his mouth.

With Pup sitting, press on both sides of his upper lip, right behind the canine teeth, using your thumb and forefinger. This will cause him to open his mouth. As soon as he does, slide the wooden dowel into his open mouth.

Pull Pup's lips back to make sure that he doesn't bite down on them when he closes his mouth. You do not want to associate pain with the act of obeying the exercise. When you're sure he won't bite his own lip, hook one finger underneath his collar, while putting your thumb in the "V" crotch underneath his chin to keep him from opening his mouth. Then give the command "hold." Hold Pup in this position so that he can't let go of the dowel and praise him. Obviously, food treats aren't going to work here.

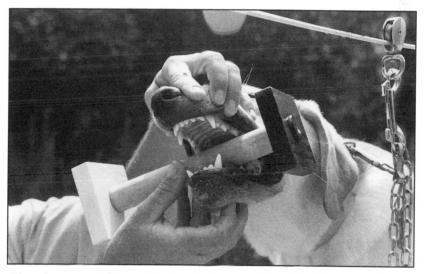

When he opens his mouth, insert the dowel, holding his upper lip clear of his teeth.

Now you want to get Pup to give you the dowel back. To do that, gently but firmly grab both ends of the dowel. Push down and roll the dowel backwards. This pries his jaw down and backwards. As you push down and roll back, Pup's mouth will open, and when it does say the command "give" and remove the dowel from his mouth.

Continue this exercise during the next several training sessions. After a few days you will find your dog holding the dowel on the command "hold," and letting you have the dowel back on the command "give."

So far you have been opening Pup's mouth by pressing behind the canine teeth. The next step in the force training is to teach him to open his mouth on his own. This is where the discomfort begins.

Force training causes discomfort, or "pressure," as trainers refer to it. The pressure is not great and it doesn't have to last long, but this training method requires pressure because an important step in force training is Pup learning how to turn off the pressure or discomfort.

To keep Pup from dropping the dowel, hold him by the collar and press your thumb or finger into the V under his chin.

Here's how you create that discomfort through the toe-pinch method. Take a string, about the size of kite string or a bit larger and tie it around Pup's front leg elbow as shown in the photo. Extend the string down that same leg to his two middle toes. Tie a half-hitch knot around those two middle toes. The area between a dog's toes is sensitive, and a slight pull on the string will cause discomfort.

Get the dowel ready, then pull the string, pinching Pup's toes and creating a bit of discomfort. When he feels the pressure he will open his mouth, in effect to say "ouch." When Pup opens his mouth, put the dowel in it and say "hold." When he holds the dowel, release the string (removing the discomfort) and praise him.

This toe-pinch has forced Pup to open his mouth and taught him that as soon as he holds the dowel, the pressure goes away.

Go slow. Too much pressure too soon could sour Pup on these training sessions.

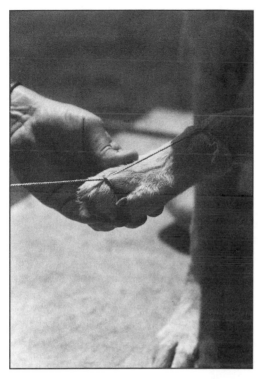

Tie the string between Pup's two middle toes.

When Pup gets it right, praise him and reward him with fun bumpers. Then end the training session for the day. You want Pup to look forward to the training sessions. He needs to know that although there may be pressure during the training, fun and rewards always follow.

If you're patient, release the pressure properly, and praise Pup when he gets that dowel in his mouth, it won't be long before you'll see your dog trying to get that dowel in his mouth on your command, before the discomfort begins.

A slight pull on the string will cause enough discomfort to make Pup open his mouth and accept the dowel.

The Next Stage

When Pup will grab the dowel on his own, it's time to add the word "fetch." This part of the exercise allows him to make the connection between "hold" and "fetch."

Hold the dowel in front of Pup's mouth. When he reaches for the dowel, command "fetch." If Pup does not take the dowel on the "fetch" command, give the "hold" command and apply the pressure of the toe-pinch. As soon as he takes the dowel, add the word "fetch" and release the pressure. Pup will soon make the connection that "fetch" and "hold" mean the same thing—and that he can turn off the pressure if he gets the dowel into his mouth when he hears the command "fetch."

Through consistency and repetition you will have a dog that will take the dowel and hold it on hearing the command "fetch." And he'll do this every time because he has been "forced." If he does not obey the command, he experiences discomfort. As soon as he obeys the command, the discomfort disappears.

Later in the book you'll see that the concept of turning off pressure will be important in reinforcing the basics using the electronic collar. The force retrieve is the introduction to the concept of learning to turn off pressure.

Reinforcing "Hold" with Distractions

You want your top dog to obey the hold command under all circumstances. You're going to create distractions to teach that. In the beginning, keep the distractions simple. Give Pup the "hold" command, and when he gets the dowel in his mouth, praise him. Then create distractions. Bang on the table. Run in circles. Speak gibberish (it's OK this time). If Pup drops the dowel without a "give" command from you, say "no" in a sharp, unhappy voice. Put him in the sit position, offer the dropped dowel, and give the "hold" command. Create distractions and continue the process. Pup will soon learn that if he drops that dowel without your "give" command, you're going to be angry.

The Ear Pinch

The toe pinch works on the force-fetch table, but when Pup is on the ground in a working situation, you won't be able to chase him around and pull a string attached to his toe. To continue the force retrieve you must be able to create discomfort while Pup is moving.

You can accomplish this through the ear pinch. Again, the idea behind this pinch is to create discomfort that Pup can turn off. The ear is a sensitive part of a dog's skin that you can reach while he is moving.

To create discomfort with the ear pinch, reach around behind Pup, as shown. Put your thumbnail against the tender underside of the ear flap and place your index finger on the outside. When you press the sharp edge of your thumbnail against the underside of the ear, you will bring discomfort to the tender underside of the ear flap.

Hold the dowel in front of him. Press your thumbnail against the inside of the ear flap and command "fetch." As soon as Pup puts the dowel in his mouth, release your thumb and stop the pressure.

Pressure from your thumbnail against the tender underside of Pup's ear will make him open his mouth and accept the dowel.

It's the same lesson as the toe pinch. You create discomfort so that the moment Pup obeys the command, the pressure goes away. Once he understands this, it will give him added confidence to know that he has the power to turn off the pressure by obeying the command.

Once you have transferred the discomfort from the toe to the ear and Pup has learned that he can turn off the pain to the ear by getting the dowel in his mouth, you're ready to start moving with the dog.

Up to this point, Pup has been on the shortened tether. Now you're going to lengthen that tether, so he will be able to walk from one end of the table to the other and retrieve the dowel anywhere along the way.

In the next part of the training, you want Pup to move a few steps in one direction and make a fetch, then move a few steps in the other direction and make a fetch. Every fetch up until now has been from your hand. In this part of the exercise, you will want him to learn to pick the dowel up from the table, not from the hand.

With Pup tethered to the cable, hold the dowel up off the table and a few feet away from Pup, toward one end of the table. Command "fetch." Apply pressure to the ear as Pup moves toward the dowel. As

The ear pinch allows you to exert pressure on Pup while he is moving.

soon as he takes the dowel in his mouth, release the pressure and praise him. If Pup does not move toward the dowel when you command "fetch," you will have to hold the dowel in one hand while pinching the ear and pulling him toward the dowel with the other hand. This can get complicated, so it's a good idea to have a helper if you run into this situation. You give the command, pinch the ear, and pull Pup along toward the dowel while your helper holds the dowel.

Each time Pup takes the dowel from your hand (or your helper's hand), praise him. The very next time you command "fetch" lower the dowel a little toward the table. The idea is to lower the dowel little by little until Pup is eventually picking the dowel up off the table.

Pup may not readily pick the dowel up off the table because this lesson is new to him. Until now, he has only taken the dowel from your hand. If he will not pick the dowel up off the table, say "fetch," apply the pressure to the ear, and touch the dowel with your other hand. Soon he should make the connection and pick the dowel off the table on his own. As always, release the ear pinch the moment he does.

As the exercise continues over a period of weeks, continue to make each retrieve a bit longer until Pup is picking the dowel up at each end of the table and giving it to you. When he reaches that stage of training, you should be able to put him in the sit position at one end of the table, place the dowel at the opposite end, and command "fetch." Pup should move to the opposite end of the table and bring you the dowel. If he doesn't, go back to the ear pinch. Soon he will get the message that he must pick up the dowel every time or the discomfort will return. Consistency is the key to making these lessons stick; don't shout at Pup or sting him with the crop one time and then return to the ear pinch. You'll only make the learning process more confusing.

When Pup is fetching consistently from both ends of the table, it's time to see if he can do the same thing on the ground. Once Pup is on the ground, the first thing you do is another exercise designed to reinforce the hold command. Just like the reinforcement command on the table, this exercise is designed to teach the dog to hold the dowel until he is given the command to release it. To teach that, you're going to ask Pup to hold the dowel while you put him through an obedience drill.

With Pup on the ground, place the dowel on the ground and command "fetch." When he gets the dowel in his mouth, put him in the sit position. If he obeys that, call him to you, then command "heel." Once he is in the "heel" position, command "sit." Step away from him and command "here." Throughout this process, Pup should obey your commands while continuing to hold the dowel. When he performs this drill consistently, it's time to move to the next lesson.

The Walking Fetch

The walking fetch transfers what Pup learned on the force-fetch table to the ground.

Place three dowels on the ground in a triangle about ten yards apart, as shown. With Pup on the leash, walk him toward one of the dowels. As you approach the dowel, command "fetch." He should pick up the dowel. When he does, command "here" and he should come toward you. When Pup approaches you, command "heel" and then "sit." When he sits, hold out your hand and command "give." Pup should open his mouth and release the dowel to your hand.

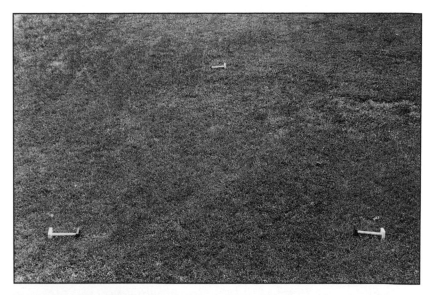

To practice the walking fetch, place three dowels on the ground in a triangle ten feet apart.

As you approach the dowel, command "fetch" and he should pick it up.

Drop the dowel behind you (so you can return to it later as you proceed around the triangle), move to the next dowel, and repeat the exercise. If your dog obeys each step of the exercise, you can be pleased. You're on your way to success.

If he does not fetch the dowel, use the ear pinch again until he picks it up and continue with the basic commands described above while he holds the dowel. If Pup does not obey the basics, you'll have to go back and work on those lessons. You cannot move forward in the training until Pup consistently obeys the basic commands.

The walking fetch is the first time Pup has been asked to put all of these behaviors together into one exercise, so don't be frustrated if it does not go perfectly the first day. Be patient. Keep working. Soon you will see it all come together.

When Pup is confident on the walking fetch using the dowel, it's time to introduce other things for him to fetch. Start with bumpers. He is familiar with bumpers from all your fun-bumper play. Lay the bumpers in a triangle as you did the dowels and repeat the exercise.

If Pup picks up the bumper, praise him and continue the exercise. If he refuses to pick up the bumper after repeated attempts, go back to the force-fetch table. Using the bumper instead of the dowel, carry out the exercise on the force-fetch table, starting with the toe-pinch. This time, however, Pup will already have an understanding of how he can turn off the pressure—so forcing him to fetch the bumper should go quickly.

When he will hold the bumper on the table, go to the ground and continue the walking fetch.

The next stage of the walking fetch is to continue the exercise with other objects Pup will be asked to retrieve—like ducks. Place three recently deceased ducks in a triangle and continue the exercise. But beware! A duck is about a thousand times more interesting to a well-bred retriever than a bumper. It is written on a retriever's DNA that fetching a duck is the most exciting thing in the world. So, be sure to use your check cord. You don't want Pup to get carried away and run off with the duck; that would set you back in your training.

Congratulations, you've taught Pup the basics. From this point on you'll learn how to reinforce those basics, and the best way to do that is through the use of the electronic collar.

• • •

PART TWO

Reinforcing the Basics
With the Electronic Collar

7
CHAPTER

Introduction to the Electronic Collar

Before you even think about using an electronic collar on your dog, burn this thought into your mind: **The electronic collar is used for one purpose in this training regimen—to reinforce behaviors the dog already knows.**

The electronic collar is a terrible way to *train* your dog, that is, to teach the basics. You do that through the lessons outlined in Part I of this book and through those shown in the *Top Dog*, *Game Dog*, and *Water Dog* videos. Do not attempt to use the electronic collar unless you're confident that Pup will respond consistently to the commands described in Part I.

Used properly, however, the electronic collar is a wonderful way to *reinforce* the basics.

In some ways the electronic collar acts as a 500- or 1,000-foot check cord. It gives you the power to reach out to a dog, even when he is well away from you, and remind him to obey a command he already knows. He knows through basic training that he can turn off discomfort by obeying the command. Any of you who have ever chased a dog across a field trying to catch him to make him obey can appreciate the potential of this long-range check cord as an effective training tool.

Many trainers once used what some called the "stomp, kick, and whip" method. Others used birdshot (at a distance) to reinforce training lessons when the dog was out of reach. The electronic collar has replaced those methods as a much more humane, controllable, and effective way to reinforce training. The discomfort created by the electronic collar is mild and it's over in the blink of an eye. It makes the whole process easier for both the trainer and the dog.

Problems created by the electronic collar are usually caused by untrained or impatient trainers. The electronic collar is never used to punish. It's never used to take out your anger and frustration on a dog you cannot control. If you want to use the electronic collar to prove to the dog that you're the boss, take this book back to the store.

But if you want to reinforce lessons your dog already knows, in a patient and consistent way, then the electronic collar is an excellent training tool that will help you produce a top dog.

What is the Electronic Collar?

Electronic collars used in dog training consist of two parts: a transmitter that you carry, which broadcasts a signal, and a small receiver that is attached to a collar the dog wears. The receiver has two metal contacts on the outside that make contact with the dog's neck and give him an electronic "sting," or stimulation, when the button is pushed on the transmitter.

Buy an electronic transmitter that is capable of delivering two types of stimulation: a continuous stimulation that continues as long as the button is held down, and a momentary stimulation (or "nick") that lasts for a very short, predetermined time. Make sure the electronic transmitter you buy automatically shuts off the continuous signal after about ten seconds. This safeguard avoids problems if the button sticks, and it is an impediment to hotheads out to punish a dog.

Most collars also allow the operator to vary the severity of the sting from a very slight tingle to a more noticeable discomfort. The level of discomfort is never enough to hurt a dog, but you can select the level that will get your dog's attention. Some models have various-colored plugs that attach to the collar; each plug delivers a different level of stimulation. Other models have a dial on the transmitter to vary the level of intensity.

Different collars will broadcast across different distances. Some will transmit 200 yards; others as far as two miles. Whichever strength transmitter you buy, it is important to never correct the dog with the collar unless you can actually see what he is doing.

To reinforce basic lessons with the electronic collar, you use the same principle you used in the toe-pinch and ear-pinch exercises. Pup learns that he can turn off the discomfort (now coming from an electronic collar rather than a pinch) by obeying the command.

Try the various models and pick the one that works best for you.

Bringing the Collar Home

When you bring your collar home, don't strap it on the dog immediately. Try it out first. There should be a test light that comes with the collar to verify that the collar is working properly; on some units the test light is a built-in LED. Push the transmitter button and the light should turn on as the signal is sent to the electrodes.

To test the collar, hold the transmitter button down. The light should come on.

Try the continuous stimulation button. Notice how the light stays on as long as you hold the button down (or until it reaches the maximum time allowed). Next, try the momentary "nick" button. Watch how the light blinks on, then off. Stimulation will be sent to the dog for the exact amount of time that the light is on. Trying out the collar before it is attached to the dog is a good way to understand how it operates without making mistakes on Pup.

Introducing Pup to the Collar

On the better models of electronic collars, there is a button on the receiver that activates the collar. Unless you push that button, the collar will not work. You want to introduce the collar to Pup with the collar not activated as he is still working on the lessons in basic training during weeks thirteen to sixteen. That way, there is no chance for you to make a mistake. This approach also gives the dog time to get used to the collar.

Strap the collar onto Pup. He should be big enough that his neck will hold up the weight of the collar during the entire training exercise. If the weight of the collar makes Pup hang his head, then he is too young for this training. Since the collar is not activated at this point, Pup's actual age is not as important as whether he is strong enough to carry the collar. (Later I'll discuss how old Pup needs to be before the collar is actually activated.)

To get Pup used to the collar, place it on him during the last few weeks of basic training.

The only purpose of putting the collar on the dog at this point is to let him get used to it around his neck while he does some of the basic training exercises. Make sure the collar is loose enough so that two

The collar should be loose enough to allow your fingers to slide underneath it.

fingers will slide easily between the dog's skin and the collar.

From now on, Pup will wear the collar during every training session. Introducing the collar now lets Pup get used to it and prevents him from becoming "collar wise" later when you begin actual lessons with the collar activated. If you were to put the collar on Pup only when you're going to use it, it would not take him long to realize that when that collar is on he has to obey you, and when the collar is not on he can do exactly as he pleases.

Never leave the collar on Pup when he is in the kennel. He should come to think of the collar as something used only during training sessions. Wearing the collar in his pen minimizes the power of the collar, and carrying around that added weight will eventually cause neck trouble.

At What Age Should You Begin Electronic Collar Training?

At what age should you activate the collar and begin reinforcing basic training? As important as that question is—nobody wants to activate the collar too soon and harm the dog—there is no one age for all dogs. Every dog is different. Introducing electronic collar training depends on when you think your dog is ready—when he is mature enough to handle the added pressure. Again, the collar should never be activated until Pup is fully versed on the basics. When he's reached that point and you are convinced he has the maturity to handle a bit more pressure it's time to begin the electronic-collar training process.

Collar Conditioning

Read the manual that came with your electronic collar and learn all you can about it, including how to activate the collar and set the levels of intensity.

You first want to establish the minimum level of intensity at which your dog will respond. To determine that level, start with the collar's lowest level. Give Pup a command that he knows. If he does not obey the command, hit the continuous button, and if he does not respond, you know he is not feeling the stimulation. Raise the level one notch and try again. Give Pup another command that he knows. If he does not respond, hit the continuous button. If you see him flinch or move in any way that indicates he felt the discomfort, that level of intensity should be enough.

The collar's intensity level should be set high enough to make Pup flinch or show some obvious sign of discomfort when you push the transmitter button, but not so high as to make him cry out.

You want Pup to get the least stimulation possible while still feeling some discomfort. Collar reinforcement is based on a dog learning that when he obeys the command, he turns off the discomfort. For this system to work, the collar has to deliver at least some discomfort or the dog will not be motivated to turn it off.

Notice I said that you needed to give the dog a command that he already knows before using the electronic collar. You don't want the stimulation of the collar coming out of nowhere. If the discomfort follows the logic of pressure Pup has already experienced, then he will accept it. By now, he is used to the sting of the training crop. You're going to build on that by transferring the sting from the crop to the stimulation from the collar.

With Pup on a leash and the crop at your side, give the "sit" command. He should know that command means "Sit now." If he does not sit the instant you give the command, sting him with the crop. He should sit right away. Lead him ahead a few yards and give the "sit" command again. This time, nick Pup with the momentary stimulation button of the electronic collar. Pup will feel the nick for about a half a second. Following the "sting" of the crop, the nick of the collar will feel familiar. He accepts it and knows what to do to avoid the discomfort.

When you see that Pup has made the connection that the discomfort of the nick is the same as the sting of the crop, then you can stop using the crop. Continue the exercise using only the collar.

If Pup shows any hesitation or confusion about the electronic collar, go back to the crop and start over. You do not want to continue with the nick of the collar until you can see that he is making the connection.

The sit command works well in transferring the sting from the crop to the collar because the crop is one small "sting" and the collar, in this instance, is one small nick. Pup is able to make the connection and accepts the nick of the collar as something he is familiar with.

But what if Pup obeys the command? You can't nick him for obeying. So what do you do? The answer depends on how quickly Pup obeys the command. "Sit" means "Sit now, no fooling around!" If you give the command and Pup does not sit right away, that is enough of a mistake to correct him. He will understand that the nick from the collar means "Hurry up and sit now." If he does sit immediately, you'll have to wait until such time as he doesn't follow a basic command or dawdles in doing so.

In the beginning, the electronic collar can be stressful to a dog. Go easy. Take your time. Make the training sessions short. And always remember to throw fun bumpers after each training session to relieve the dog's stress.

• • •

CHAPTER

Reinforcing the Basics

This chapter will show you how to use the electronic collar to reinforce the basic "sit," "here," "heel," and "fetch" commands.

In effect, all of the more advanced lessons we will explore in the following chapters are based on these basic commands. As you'll soon learn, when you send your dog off on an exercise called "force to the pile," he will actually be performing a compilation of "sit," "here," "heel," and "fetch." If Pup is not well schooled in those basics, he will not be able to carry out the exercises I'll cover in the following chapters.

For a retriever to be a top dog he must have ingrained in his psyche the desire to obey the basic commands every time, no matter what the circumstances. The electronic collar gives you the power to create that desire to obey commands without hesitation or second thoughts. I know a jet pilot in the Air Force. He told me that pilots are taught to perform certain procedures so thoroughly that when they are under pressure they don't even have to think about them. They know exactly what to do. They react immediately. That's how you want these basics lessons ingrained in your retriever.

At this point in the training, Pup should have been wearing the electronic collar, during the training sessions only, for at least a month. You have transferred the sting from the training crop to the sting of the collar and Pup is familiar with the discomfort the collar delivers.

Reinforcing "Sit"

You will use the continuous button on the electronic collar to reinforce "sit." At this point, Pup knows the voice command for "sit." He also knows that the whistle command for "sit" is one sharp blast.

With Pup on a leash and the collar set at the same intensity level you've already been using, walk him in your training area and command "sit." As soon as you get the "sit" command out of your mouth, hit the continuous stimulation button. Pup should begin to sit immediately. Your first reaction may be to let off the button the moment your dog *begins* to sit. Don't do it. "Sit" means "Get your butt on the ground now." Hold the continuous stimulation button until the moment Pup's butt hits the ground, then release it. Praise him and continue.

"Sit" means "Sit right now." Hold the continuous pressure button until Pup's butt touches the ground.

By applying continuous pressure and releasing the pressure only when the dog fully obeys the command, you're letting Pup in on the game. He gets to participate. It is a bit like the old television game *Beat the Clock*. Pup obeys the command as fast as he can to turn off the stimulation. He learns that he is in control of the situation, which is why this method keeps him confident and happy.

Reinforcing the "Sit" Whistle Command

To reinforce the whistle command, walk Pup on the leash. Give the whistle command for "sit," one short blast on the whistle. A split second after you whistle the command, hit the continuous stimulation button. The moment Pup's butt hits the ground, release the button. Praise him.

Praise Pup each time he successfully completes a task.

Do this three or four times, and then throw fun bumpers and quit for the day.

If your dog reacts in a negative way to the continuous button, go back to the crop and use the momentary stimulation to recondition him to the collar. In any of the collar reinforcement exercises, you may find that use of the continuous stimulation button causes Pup to freeze up or stand motionless. This means one of two things: either Pup does not understand what you want or the intensity level on the collar is too high. If this situation occurs, lower the intensity level and see if that corrects the problem. You shouldn't have the problem in the first place if you start with the lowest level of intensity and work your way up if needed.

A note about when to hit the continuous button: Some trainers hit the button a split second before giving the command. Others give the command first, then immediately hit the button. Most of the trainers I have observed give the command and hit the continuous button a split second afterward; that's the method I'd suggest you use.

Reinforcing the "Here" Voice Command

Since you've taken the careful steps to introduce your dog to the electronic collar on "sit," he should now have learned that he has the power to turn off the pressure by obeying the command. This makes reinforcing "here" and "heel" a faster process.

"Here" means "Come here now." To give the command, say the dog's name first, followed by "here" or "come" (whichever command you have consistently been using). The moment you get the command out of your mouth, hit the continuous stimulation button. As soon as Pup begins to come to you, release the pressure. This is slightly different than applying pressure for "sit," where you did not release the pressure until Pup fully obeyed the command and his butt hit the ground. With the "here" command, release the pressure as soon as he commits to move toward you.

So far you have been reinforcing all these commands with the dog on a leash or check cord. "Here" is no different. For the "here" command, start with Pup on a twenty-five-foot check cord.

Give the command, apply continuous pressure with the electronic collar, and release the pressure when Pup starts toward you. Don't pull the check cord as soon as you give the command; you want Pup to obey the command because he understands it, not because

"Here" means "Come here now." When you give the "here" command, apply continuous stimulation with the collar until Pup turns and starts to move toward you.

you're pulling on the check cord. In the event that he does not obey the command, even with continuous pressure, you have the check cord as a tool to assist you. Say the dog's name, give the "here" command, apply continuous pressure from the collar, and pull Pup toward you with the check cord. When he commits to run toward you, release the button and the pressure.

A word of warning: If Pup will not obey the "here" command, even with the pressure of the collar, you may not have laid the groundwork properly in teaching the basics. If you think that is the case, go back and start over; teaching the "here" command with the check cord and no electronic collar.

If you're convinced Pup knows the command but still will not obey, even with the continuous stimulation of the collar, he may be freezing because the intensity level on the collar is set too high. Reduce the intensity level and try again.

Reinforcing the "Here" Whistle Command

The whistle command for "here" is one long blast, a sound that seems to say "heeerrrrre." To reinforce that command, blow the whistle command for "here," then apply continuous pressure with the collar. As soon as Pup commits to move toward you, release the pressure. If he still does not obey, whistle the "here" command again, apply continuous pressure, and pull him toward you with the check cord. When he commits to run toward you, release the pressure.

When Pup successfully obeys the whistle command for "here" three or four times, throw fun bumpers and quit training for the day. Never overdo it. You always want your dog to feel that these training sessions are fun. There will be pressure from time to time, but the sessions should never be overly long and they should always end on the upbeat exercise of fun bumpers.

Mistakes Are a Trainer's Best Friend

Mistakes are a good opportunity to reinforce a training lesson using the electronic collar. Pup may not make mistakes obeying "here" on a short leash, but put him at a greater distance from you on a long check cord and chances are greater that he'll not consistently obey the command. If he fails to come to the voice or whistle command immediately, apply continuous pressure. When he begins to come toward you, release the pressure.

When Pup always obeys, even at the end of a long check cord, graduate to a more challenging situation. Take him off the check cord, but make sure he's in a fenced-in training area like a little league baseball park. Let him run. When you know he can hear you, say his name, followed immediately by the "here" voice or whistle command. If he fails to come immediately, apply continuous pressure and release it as soon as he makes his move toward you.

If Pup will not come to you even when continuous pressure is applied, either he doesn't feel it or he doesn't know what you want. The electronic stimulation must be great enough for him to want to get rid of it. If he doesn't understand what behavior you expect, take the collar off and go back to basics.

Reinforcing "Heel"

When you call Pup's name and he comes in to you, it should become automatic for you to put him in the heel position. "Heel" means that Pup must put his butt at your heel as fast as possible. It is an important command because it allows you to position Pup where you want him. You use the heel command to move him from one area and to line him up in a new direction.

To reinforce "heel" with the electronic collar, begin with Pup on a check cord some ten feet ahead of you in a remote sit position. Give the "heel" command, and the moment the command comes out of your mouth, hit the continuous stimulation button. Do not release the continuous button until Pup fully obeys the command. Heel does not mean "sort of heel." It means "Come here and get your butt at my heel immediately." When Pup has done that, release the continuous button. Reinforce "heel" three or four times, then end the training session.

If Pup moves ahead or lags behind, command "heel" and press the continuous stimulation button until he returns to the heel position.

The Moving Heel

The moving heel is simply when your dog stays in the heel position while you are walking. You'd use this command, for example, when you take Pup out of the truck and walk him toward the blind.

To reinforce the moving heel: With Pup on the check cord, heel him at your side and begin to walk. If he moves ahead of you, repeat the command "heel" and immediately hit the continuous button and pull him toward you with the check cord while you continue to walk. When Pup moves back into the heel position, release the electronic stimulation. Likewise, if Pup lags behind, repeat the "heel" command, apply continuous pressure and pull him toward you until he completely obeys the command, and then release the button.

When you feel Pup is well reinforced in the stationary and moving "heel" commands, try a training session where you reinforce both. This is stressful work; don't overdo it. And always end with the joy of fun bumpers.

Debolting

When a dog "bolts," it means he runs away to avoid the pressure. I understand this because I do the same thing. When I'm under the pressure of a work deadline, I call people, clean the office, sharpen pencils—anything to avoid the task at hand. What makes me come back and deal with the pressure of work is the bill collector. I know that the only way to get rid of paying the bills is to return to work and finish it. But a dog does not know he has to come back. He just wants to get away from the pressure. You must drill it into your dog that he cannot run away to avoid the pressure. You do this with the debolting exercise.

Under too much pressure a dog will escape to a safe haven. Near home, it may be his kennel. In the field, it may be the safety of his dog box. If a family member is nearby, he may want to run to them. It's a good idea to work on debolting in an area where the dog has a safe haven nearby. For the purposes of this example, let's use the area around your dog's kennel.

When pressured, a dog will attempt to escape to a safe haven. Do not correct him when he's running; make him sit first, then correct him.

When Pup bolts, stop him with the "sit" command and correct him with the collar.

After he sits, command heel and apply continuous pressure with the collar...

To put pressure on Pup, start with the walking heel. Bring him into the heel position and begin to walk. If he gets ahead of you or lags behind, command "heel" and hit the continuous button. If he returns to the heel position, release the continuous button.

If Pup bolts, however, do not immediately use the electronic collar to correct him. You never want to correct Pup "on the fly." There are too many variables—too much is going on—when a dog is moving. He is unlikely to know

...until he returns to your side.

what the corrective stimulation of the collar means. Before you correct the moving dog with the collar, you stop him with a whistle blast, put him in the sit position, and then correct with the collar. Because the collar correction does not take place the moment the dog makes the mistake, this is called indirect pressure.

Now let's look at how to correct debolting using indirect pressure.

Walk Pup in the moving heel with no check cord attached. If he were on a check cord, he could not bolt. In this case, you want him to bolt so you can correct him. When Pup moves away from the heel position, command "heel" and apply continuous pressure until he returns to the heel position.

If Pup bolts (runs away), correct him in the following manner: The moment he makes the mistake, command "sit." If you've laid the groundwork on the basics, he should sit. With Pup in the sitting position, facing you, shout a sharp, unhappy "no," nick him with the momentary button. Follow that nick with another sharp "no." Then pause for a moment, long enough to give him a chance to consider what he did and to realize that you are unhappy. When you think he has had time to let that sink in, repeat the "heel" command. The moment the command is out of your mouth, hit the continuous stimulation button. Pup should start toward you, returning to the heel position. Hold the continuous button down until he has fully obeyed the command by completely returning to the heel position.

If you correct the dog with the collar while he is in the act of running away, what some call "burn on the fly," you are only taking out your anger and frustration on the dog. This will confuse the dog and set him back in his training. A good trainer handles a situation in such a way that the dog understands what the trainer wants.

To review debolting: The moment Pup bolts, put him in the sit position with either the voice or whistle command. Think of the sit position as a student seated at his desk at school. Think of yourself as the teacher seating the student to make him listen. With the student at his desk, looking at you and listening, shout a sharp, unhappy "no," nick the dog with the momentary stimulation button, and repeat "no." If you stopped Pup with the "sit" command earlier—the moment he began to bolt—then he will understand what you are unhappy about.

After giving Pup time to consider what he did wrong, repeat the "heel" command. As soon as the command is out of your mouth, hit the continuous button and hold it down until Pup fully obeys the command by returning to the heel position.

Bolting does not only happen on the moving heel. Any time you put pressure on the dog to obey a command and he attempts to run away, use this same approach to stop him, correct him, and force him obey your command using the "long leash" of the electronic collar.

Reinforcing the Force Retrieve

The force retrieve is based on the continuous pressure of the toe pinch and the ear pinch. At this point in the training, Pup already understands that getting the bumper in his mouth turns off the pressure of the toe pinch and picking up the dumbbell from the force-fetch table stops the pressure of the ear pinch. Now you will teach Pup that fully obeying the force retrieve commands will stop the pressure of the electronic collar.

Before you begin with the collar, you need to transfer the discomfort from the toe pinch and the ear pinch to the electronic collar. Let's start with the toe pinch.

Put Pup back on the force-fetch table, just as you did in the earlier chapter on force retrieving. Tighten the tether from his collar to the overhead line so that he cannot move his head to escape the pressure.

Hold the bumper out in front of Pup, give the command "hold," and apply pressure. As soon as he gets the bumper in his mouth, release the pressure of the toe pinch, exactly as you did in the earlier lessons. By getting the bumper in his mouth, Pup got rid of the discomfort of the toe pinch.

Now, substitute the pressure of the electronic collar for the toe pinch. Again, loosen the tether, place a bumper at one end of the table, and walk Pup down the force-fetch table to the bumper and show it to him. Move to the other end of the table, take Pup by the collar, and lead him down the table toward the bumper. As you near the bumper, give the "fetch" command. As soon as you say "fetch," hit the continuous button *as you continue to lead Pup toward the bumper*. He'll pick up the bumper if he makes the connection that he can end the stimulation by doing so. If he balks or will not move, he likely has not yet made the connection; go back to the ear pinch. Lead Pup toward the bumper, give the "fetch" command, and pinch his ear. He will pick up the bumper to rid himself of the pressure of the ear pinch.

Place the bumper back on the table, move to the other end of the table with the dog, and repeat the "fetch" command. Press the continuous button and hold it down while leading Pup to the bumper. If he still does not understand what you want, stop. Pick up the bumper and hold it in front

Stimulation from the electronic collar takes the place of the toe pinch and the ear pinch. Release the continuous stimulation button when Pup picks up the bumper.

of him. Give the "fetch" command and hit the continuous button. While holding the continuous button down, put the bumper in his mouth. (You may need an assistant.) When the bumper is in his mouth, release the button to turn off the pressure.

It shouldn't take an intelligent dog long to realize that he can get rid of the discomfort of the collar by picking up the bumper. When Pup makes that association, it's time to reinforce the walking fetch.

Command "fetch" and hit the continuous button.

Release the button as soon as Pup picks up the bumper.

Reinforcing the Walking Fetch

The walking fetch should have already been taught using the ear pinch and the training crop.

To reinforce the walking fetch with the electronic collar, take Pup off the table and work with him on the ground. Place five bumpers in a line, each ten to fifteen feet apart. Put your dog into the heel position, then command "sit." While he is in the sit position facing the line of bumpers, command "fetch." The

Take the bumper from him and send him to fetch the next in line.

goal is to have Pup fetch the first bumper and return it to you. As he returns the bumper, take it from him, drop it behind you, and step forward as you command him to "fetch" the next bumper in the line. The first step is to have Pup retrieve a whole line of bumpers, using only the training crop, if necessary.

Let's review how you use the crop on this exercise, and then I'll show you how to transfer the sting of the crop to the collar. With Pup in the sit position facing the line of bumpers, command "fetch." As he moves to fetch the first bumper, sting him with the crop. Use the crop lightly, giving just enough bite to goose him along. Once he has picked up the whole line of bumpers, repeat the exercise, this time replacing the sting of the crop with the electronic collar.

With Pup in the sit position facing the line of bumpers, command "fetch." The moment the command is out of your mouth, hit the continuous button. Pup should run to the bumper. As soon as he gets it in his mouth, release the button. Like the sting of the crop, the stimulation from the collar means "Hurry up, get it now." When Pup realizes that he can get rid of the stimulation by picking up the bumper, he will retrieve the bumper as fast as he can. When he will pick up a line of bumpers every time, he's ready for the next exercise.

• • •

9
CHAPTER

The Blind Retrieve

I talked about marks and blinds in an earlier chapter. A mark is a bird or a bumper that a dog sees go down. A blind is a bird or bumper that he doesn't see go down. To run a blind, your dog depends on you to guide him to the bird or bumper. Running a blind is an absolute requirement for a top dog.

A mark is a bumper, and later a bird, that Pup sees fall.

The first step in learning to run a blind is an exercise called "force to the pile." The pile in this exercise is literally a pile of bumpers. In force to the pile, you guide Pup to that pile of bumpers and have him retrieve one. It's the first building block in teaching him to leave your side, go into a field or water, follow your directions to find a bumper or a bird that he never saw fall, and bring it to you.

Teaching Pup to run a blind requires a new set of lessons, but they are built on the basics you've already taught—"sit," "here," "heel" and "fetch." To run a blind, Pup has to line up in the direction you establish, leave your side, and move straight along that line. The accuracy of the line is important. When you command "here" and pivot to his left, Pup will pivot to his left. When you command "heel" and pivot to the right, Pup will pivot to the right.

To run a blind retrieve, Pup will learn to leave your side on the command "back," which you'll teach him based on the "fetch" command. You'll also teach him to sit at a distance—the "remote sit"—based on the simple "sit" command.

Then your dog will need to know how to continue beyond the remote sit and to make "directional backs," spinning in one direction or the other to cast back at an angle. He will also learn "overs," casting to one side or the other. Finally, once he finds the blind, he must be able to retrieve it straight back to you; that ability is based on the "fetch" and "here" commands.

With the blind retrieve you'll start to see your work on the basics come together in performance that is the mark of a top dog.

Force to the Pile

Place a pile of ten bumpers ten to fifteen yards from where Pup will begin the exercise. Pick a distance you are confident he can retrieve from successfully. The number of bumpers really doesn't matter, but it needs to be enough to make the pile clearly visible to Pup. All of the bumpers should be white.

With one bumper in hand, call Pup to you. Heel him and put him in the sit position facing the pile. To make sure he is watching what you're about to do, command "mark," which means "Heads up. Something is about to happen." When you're sure Pup is watching, toss the bumper onto the pile. Since Pup saw the bumper go down, this bumper is a mark. Release Pup to retrieve the mark by saying his name. If trained properly in the earlier lessons, he will go to the pile, get the bumper, and bring it to you.

Since Pup saw the first bumper thrown, you released him on his name. From this point on, however, you will not throw the bumper. You're going to ask him to go to the pile and bring you a bumper that he did not see thrown. That means that the rest of the bumpers in the pile are blinds. This is the beginning of teaching the command "back."

At this point in the training Pup understands the command "fetch." Now you're going to transfer the meaning of "fetch" to "back."

Force to the Pile: Step One

With Pup in the sit position facing the pile, identify the pile by throwing a bumper to it. Release him on the "fetch" command.

When he brings you the bumper, heel him and put him in the sit position. Identify the pile again, this time using the phrase "dead bird." "Dead bird" means "Heads up, something is about to happen." When you've said "dead bird" and you have his attention, toss a bumper onto the pile again and command "fetch." When Pup returns with the bumper, take it from him and praise him.

Something new is about to happen. At this point, Pup knows where the pile is located. He knows that you want him to retrieve from that pile on the command "fetch." This time you're going to ask him to go to the pile and retrieve a bumper that was not thrown. This will be the dog's first step in learning to make a blind retrieve.

Line your dog up with the pile, which is some ten yards away. Give the heads-up command of "dead bird" and release him with the command "back."

At this point, Pup has never heard the word "back," but he knows you praise him when he retrieves a bumper from the pile. He also knows "dead bird" means something is about to happen. When you give the command "back," instead of "fetch," *using the same tone of voice*, Pup is likely to go to the pile and retrieve a bumper. Tone of voice is often as important as the word; in this case it helps him make the association. When you reinforce his behavior with praise, he soon comes to realize that "back" means the same thing as "fetch."

If Pup does not make that connection, start with the word "fetch" and add "back." Toss the bumper to the pile; this is a mark, so "fetch" is enough. When he returns, line him up with the pile, then command "fetch—back." He should soon make the connection.

When he does, send him to the pile a few more times using only the "back" command. Praise him each time he gets it right. Once he's done the exercise successfully a few times, put him away for the day.

If Pup does not make the connection between "fetch" and "back," you have to let him know exactly what you want. To do that, go back to the ear pinch. Line him up with the pile at heel and command "dead bird—back!" The moment you say the word "back," pinch his ear with your thumbnail while moving him toward the pile. As soon as he gets a bumper in his mouth, release the pinch. Reward him with praise.

Once Pup has gotten it right using the ear pinch, try it again *without* the ear pinch. If he still does not understand, keep going back to the ear pinch until he makes the connection that "back" means "Leave my side now, go to the pile, and fetch a bumper."

Force to the Pile: Step Two

The "back" command doesn't mean "Go to the pile and bring me a bumper whenever you feel like it." It means "Go now and make the retrieve with style and momentum." The electronic collar is a great tool to help your dog do just that. Again, it is used as a sort of invisible training crop to urge the dog along with speed and style.

In this case you use the momentary stimulation to "nick" Pup and encourage him to pick up his pace toward the pile. This is not the continuous pressure he has to turn off.

Line up Pup with the pile. With him at heel, throw a bumper to identify the pile. Since he saw the bumper go down, making that bumper a mark, command "fetch."

Once he makes the retrieve, you're going to ask him to go back to the pile and retrieve a bumper he did not see thrown. Since that bumper will be a blind, you'll use the command "back."

Line Pup up with the pile, command "dead bird—back." He should leave your side and run for the pile of bumpers. When he is at the halfway point—the cross-over—repeat the command "back" and urge him along with a nick (momentary stimulation) from the collar. You should notice that he picks up his speed.

To increase Pup's momentum, "nick" him with the collar when he is about halfway to the pile. You should notice him pick up speed.

Force to the pile is one of the building blocks of running a blind, and you will do it over and over to get a top dog. The danger with any exercise you repeat so often is that the dog loses momentum and drive. The nick on the way to the pile picks up that momentum.

Do not, however, nick Pup every time you force him to the pile. At first, use the nick every fourth time or so. You have to nick him at this stage even if he appears to be working hard to ingrain this stimulation. After he is aware that he can be hurried along on the way to the pile, it is only necessary to nick him when he's loafing or not giving his best effort.

When Pup is forcing to the pile with style, it's time to increase the distance.

If you started with your first blind retrieves at fifteen yards, lengthen it to twenty-five yards. Follow the same steps as outlined above. Start with the mark and then go to the blind. Pup should leave your side on the command "back." If you want to say "dead bird" and then "back" every time for consistency, that's fine. "Dead bird" means "Heads up, something is about to happen." "Back" means "Leave my side and move with style and momentum in the direction

I have sent you." Don't slur the two commands together; they mean two different things. Whether you use "dead bird" every time or not, always say "back" in a clear and concise manner and remember that tone of voice matters.

End every session with praise and fun bumpers. And always try to end each session when Pup's doing the lesson right.

Force to the Pile: Step Three

To begin Step Three, set a pile of bumpers out as far as you can throw one. The reason the pile can only be as far as you can throw is that you must throw the first bumper to mark the pile.

Heel Pup to your side, facing the pile. Identify the pile by throwing the first bumper to the pile. Say the dog's name and he should retrieve the mark from the pile. At this point, the pile has become a pile of blinds. Line Pup up with the pile and command "back!" He should go to the pile with style and bring you a bumper. Force to the pile at this distance for the remainder of this training step.

Force to the Pile: Step Four

The goal here is to increase the length of the exercise. Set the pile out as far as you can throw, as in the previous step. Throw the first bumper to mark the pile. Command the dog's name. As soon as he leaves your side to retrieve the mark, move back twenty to thirty yards. When Pup returns, take the mark from him, drop it behind you, and send him with the "back" command to the pile. Using this approach, you were able to identify the pile with the mark while also lengthening the exercise for the blind retrieve.

Each time you send Pup back to the pile, step back another ten yards until you're sending him to a pile that's one hundred yards distant. Obviously, you are not required to go from thirty yards to a hundred yards on the first day. Use common sense and your dog's progress to judge how long you stay on Step Four.

Use the electronic collar's momentary nick every fourth time or so as Pup runs to the pile. Use it more often if you think he's not giving his best. As always, the nick should come at approximately the halfway point on the way to the pile. Don't nick Pup too often or you'll create a problem called "popping," which I'll discuss later in the book.

When you've completed the forcing to the pile at these longer distances, and Pup is showing energy, confidence, and enthusiasm, it's time to move on to the next exercise.

When Pup leaves to make the retrieve, move back 20 to 30 yards to increase the distance of each successive retrieve.

The Remote Sit

The remote sit is another building block in the all-important task of running a blind retrieve. As mentioned earlier, the remote sit is your classroom desk. You do not correct your student when he is on the run. You must sit him at his desk and make him listen to your commands. That "desk" is the remote sit.

Pup must learn that on hearing the remote sit command he must turn, face you, and wait for further instructions.

By now Pup should obey the "sit" command every time you give it. You'll need a twenty-five-foot check cord and a pair of gloves for this lesson. Line Pup up with the pile and command "back." He will run for the pile, and just before he reaches the halfway point, blow the whistle command for "sit." Time the command so that immediately after you deliver it, Pup hits the end of the check cord. The check cord will bring him to an instant stop and spin him around facing you. Use

When Pup reaches the end of the check cord, stop him with the whistle command for sit...

...hit the continuous button on the transmitter until his butt touches the ground.

this method two or three times; by then Pup should understand that the whistle means turn to you and sit. If he still doesn't understand, you have a tool—the electronic collar—to take it one step further.

With Pup on the check cord, line him up with the pile of bumpers. Send him to the pile with the "back" command. When he hits the end of the cord somewhere near the halfway point to the pile, blow the whistle command for "sit." At the same moment you blow the whistle, hit the continuous button on the electronic collar. If Pup has been properly collar-conditioned, he will sit immediately to stop the stimulation. As always, the moment his butt hits the ground, release the button.

Continue the exercise until Pup will stop on the whistle command for "sit," turn to you, and await further instructions. Once he will go into the remote sit consistently without the use of the check cord, throw fun bumpers and stop training for the day.

The next step in the exercise is for Pup to go into the remote sit on the return from the pile. This lesson should go a little easier because he already knows the meaning of the remote sit.

Line Pup up with the pile. Send him to the pile on the command "back." Let him get a bumper from the pile, and at the halfway point of his return, blow the whistle "sit" command. Pup should stop and sit immediately.

If he doesn't, reinforce the whistle command with the collar. Send him to the pile on the "back" command. Let him get a bumper, and on his return, blow the whistle command for sit and *immediately* hit the continuous button on the collar. He will sit to stop the stimulation. The moment his butt hits the ground, release the button. To bring him the rest of the way in, give the whistle or voice command for "here."

At this point, you have Pup retrieving the mark on the sound of his name. He is also making blind retrieves on the "back" command. He understands the remote sit on the way to the pile and on the return from it.

Now that you are able to make the dog sit in his school desk and listen, you

Pup should sit, turn to you, and await further instructions.

need to give him further direction about where to find the bird. The first direction you taught him was to leave your side on the command "back," moving in a straight line.

The next command to move in a certain direction will be to cast back. You teach this from the remote sit. Walk Pup at heel to the halfway, or crossover, point. Sit him there so that he is facing you when you step back to direct him. Throw a bumper to the pile—over Pup's head and behind his back—to identify the pile. With Pup looking at you awaiting further instructions, command "back." He should turn, go to the pile, and pick up a bumper. This is the first step in casting back from a remote sit.

Reinforcing the Cast Back from a Remote Sit

When you're sure Pup understands what you want when you give him the command to cast back, here's how you can use the electronic collar to reinforce that command.

With Pup at your side, line him up with the pile and send him to the pile using the "back" command. At the halfway point, blow the whistle command for "sit," putting him into the remote sit. With Pup sitting and facing you, raise your hand directly over your head, and command "back." He should turn, go back to the pile, and fetch a bumper. If he does not obey the command, repeat the "sit" command and, with Pup facing you, repeat the "back" command. The moment you get the "back" command out of your mouth, hit the continuous button on the electronic collar. As soon as Pup stands and turns to head for the pile, release the button. As always, if he does not know what you want, the electronic collar will not help. But if he knows what "back" means, the collar will work well here to reinforce the command.

When you have Pup consistently casting back to the pile from the remote sit without the use of the electronic collar, you're ready to introduce overs.

Teaching Overs: Step One

On a blind retrieve you want Pup to leave your side and move in a straight line. If he gets out in front of you a ways and drifts off course, you must be able to stop him and send him in the proper direction.

The "back" command sent Pup from the remote sit in a backward direction. Overs send him from the remote sit to one side or another; they cast him over to the right or over to the left.

Before you can use the electronic collar to reinforce the over command, you must teach Pup to run "overs." As you know by now, the electronic collar is only used to reinforce lessons that have already been learned.

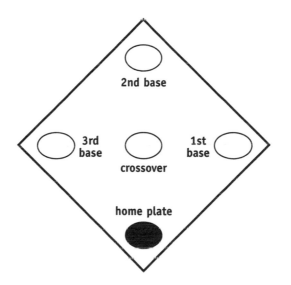

A good way to visualize the basic "t" pattern for "overs" is as a baseball diamond.

To teach overs, you're going to work on a paradigm that looks like a baseball diamond, sometimes referred to as the "t" pattern (see the diagram). The pitcher's mound would be the halfway point between home plate and second base, also called the crossover point. This is the spot where the dog will cross over to the right or to the left.

Eventually, you'll work with a pile of bumpers at first, second, and third bases. Begin, however, with a pile of bumpers on second base only. That's the pile straight away from you that Pup is used to.

With both you and Pup on home plate, bring him into the heel position, line him up with the pile on second base, and command "back." He should leave your side and run in the direction in which you lined him up. When he is halfway to the pile, whistle the "sit" command. Pup should turn to you and sit.

With Pup sitting and facing you at the crossover, toss a bumper to your right—what would be first base on a baseball diamond. You are throwing a single bumper; there is no pile there yet. Pup should watch the bumper fall but not move to retrieve it. When he looks to you for direction, lean out, exaggerating your body language as shown in the photograph, and signal him with your right arm as you command "over." This is the first time Pup has heard the command "over," but he may understand immediately what you want. Retrievers are smart, and body language means a lot to them. If Pup makes the retrieve, take the bumper from him and praise him.

Command "over" and lean toward the bumper tossed to first base, signaling Pup with your right arm.

Don't worry if he does not make the retrieve. Remember, until now he has been taught to sit until he hears his name, the command "back, " or the command "fetch." If he doesn't make a connection with "over," return to the "fetch" command. Call him back to home plate and line him up with the pile on second base. Command "back." When he is at the halfway point, blow the whistle to put him into the remote sit. While he is looking to you for further direction, toss a bumper out to first base, lean out, point to first base, and command "fetch." Pup should get the bumper and bring it to you.

Try it again using the "fetch" command. Once Pup is having fun with this, lean out using the same body language and tone of voice as you give the command "over." Keep doing the exercise, blending "fetch" with "over" until you are using the "over" command exclusively.

Once Pup has picked up his first over and returned it to you, continue this exercise two to three times. Then send him on a "back" to second base. Returning to an exercise Pup is already familiar with helps bolster his confidence.

When Pup is casting with confidence to first base, change the direction to the imaginary third base. With your dog in the heel position, line him up with the pile of bumpers on second base. Send him to the pile, using the command "back." When he reaches the halfway point, blow the whistle to put him into the remote sit. With Pup facing you awaiting further instructions, toss a bumper to third base. Lean out, exaggerating your body language, point to third base, and command "over." He should fetch the bumper from third base and bring it to you. Continue this exercise to third base, blending "fetch—over" with the "over" command if you need to get Pup to understand. For every two or three times you go to third base, send him back to the more familiar second base.

When Pup is going to first and third bases with confidence, break it up. Send him to first base a couple of times, followed by the more familiar second base, and finally to third base. Mix up the rotation. Throw some fun bumpers and quit for the day, while Pup is still retrieving enthusiastically.

To send Pup to third base, command "over," lean your body toward third, and extend your left arm.

Teaching Overs: Step Two

For the final step of teaching overs, leave the pile of bumpers at second base. Add a pile of bumpers at first base and at third base.

It is important to separate the piles in such a way that the dog will not confuse the pile at first base for the pile at second base. You don't want to send Pup on a "back" to second base, only to have him run to first base because it's closer. Spread the piles out to avoid confusion.

With piles on first, second, and third bases, send Pup back several times to second base. This gets him used to going to the more familiar second base while avoiding the lure of the closer first or third base. If he does take a detour to first or third base, however, you have an important training opportunity!

Correct Pup like this: The moment he makes the mistake, blow a sharp whistle for "sit" so that he goes into a remote sit. When he is seated and facing you, shout "no" in a harsh, unhappy tone. Then nick him with the momentary button on the collar, say "no" again in a sharp tone, and call him to you. With Pup at your side, line him up again with second base and command "back." If he makes a mistake again, correct him in the same manner. He will soon understand what he is doing wrong and will correct the behavior.

As you've learned, correcting the dog in this manner is called indirect pressure. You will use it again and again, and the procedure is always the same. "Sit" the dog, tell him "no," nick him with the electronic collar, tell him "no" again in an unhappy tone, call him in, and make him do it again.

At this point, Pup can be forced to the pile at second base. He will obey the remote sit, and from there he will cast "over" to first base and third base and "back" to second base. Now it's time to run Pup through a field check.

The Field Check

The field check is an exercise you use to make sure Pup will cast over and back—again and again, every time you ask him. This time you will ask him to cast over and back while carrying a bumper in his mouth. Until now you've sent Pup to a pile to retrieve a bumper. Now you want him to go to a pile not to retrieve a bumper but just because you told him to go there.

With piles at first, second, and third bases, heel Pup at home plate. Hold a bumper in front of him and command "fetch." He should take the bumper in his mouth. Line him up with the second base and cast him back to the pile there, using the "back" command. When he reaches the back pile, blow the whistle command for "sit." Pup should go into the remote sit.

Now you're going to ask him to cast back even farther. To do this, raise one hand high over your head and command "back." He should cast back beyond the second base pile. Blow the whistle command for "sit." He should sit.

With Pup looking to you for further instructions, give the hand signal for him to cast back, then command "back." He should cast back even farther. Sit him again with the whistle. Blow the whistle to call him in and when he is at the crossover, blow the "sit" whistle command to put him in the remote sit.

Using hand signals and the "over" command, cast Pup to the third base pile. When he reaches the pile, whistle him into a remote sit.

Using hand signals and the "over" command, send Pup beyond the third base pile. Put him into the remote sit. Give the hand signal to cast to the first base pile and command "over." When he reaches the first base pile, whistle him into the remote sit. Then cast him beyond the first base pile.

Whistle Pup into a remote sit, call him in, praise him, throw fun bumpers and end training for the day.

Cast Pup back beyond second base and have him sit and wait for further instructions.

The Directional Back

At this point, Pup is running a pattern similar to a lowercase "t"— straight back or to the left and right sides. Now it's time teach him to cast at an angle. This is called a directional back.

The goal of the blind retrieve is for Pup to retrieve a bird or bumper that he did not see go down. To do that, you must be able to send Pup in any direction, at any angle. The directional back gives you the ability to thread the needle and put your retriever exactly where he needs to be to find the bird.

To teach Pup to angle back, you must teach him to spin in the proper direction.

Pup is in the remote sit, facing you. The blind bumper is hidden in the grass, behind the dog and over his left shoulder. If you simply sent him back, he might spin to his right and miss the blind. Your goal, in this instance, would be to get the dog to cast back by spinning to his left so that he is naturally angling back in the direction of the blind.

To teach Pup to spin back to his left or his right, put him into the remote sit. With the dog facing you, exaggerate your body language and lean in the direction you want him to spin. The trick here is to try to get him to lean in the same direction you are leaning.

Let's say you want Pup to spin to *his* left. That means, facing the dog, you need to lean to *your* right. When he is leaning in the direction you're leaning, raise your right hand at an angle, as shown in the photos, and command "back." Pup should turn to run backwards, and as he turns, he is likely to spin in the direction he was leaning. Eventually he will spin in the proper direction simply because he understands the direction you want based on your hand signal. But for

Lean in the direction you want Pup to lean. Raise your hand at an angle and command "back."

Pup should spin in the direction he was leaning. Now try it in the other direction.

now, it helps to use this leaning trick before giving the hand signal and the voice command.

Once Pup seems to understand what you want when you use the leaning technique, do the spin drill without leaning. To direct Pup to spin to *his* left, for example, raise your right arm and give the "back" command. If Pup spins in the wrong direction here's how to correct it:

With Pup in the remote sit facing you, raise your right arm up at an angle, and command "back." When he spins to his right (the wrong direction) rather than his left, stop him with the "sit" command. When he sits, give him a harsh "no." By this time in the training, he should know very well what "no" means.

When this "no" has had a moment to sink in, face him, raise your right arm again, and command "back." If he spins back in the wrong direction once more, stop him again with the "sit" whistle. Shout "no!" and then step back, raise your right arm, and command "back." If he spins in the proper direction, praise him. If he spins in the wrong direction, stop him with the "sit" whistle and repeat the process.

If Pup continues to spin in the wrong direction, it's likely he doesn't fathom what you want. Go back to leaning toward the direction in which you want him to spin before you give the "back" command. Keep in mind that some dogs don't have great eyesight. Move in close enough so you're sure Pup can clearly see the hand signal.

If Pup continues to spin in the wrong direction, make every effort to correct the problem with the indirect pressure of sitting him and giving a harsh "no." If he refuses to turn in the correct direction after several lessons, then you correct him using indirect pressure and the nick of the collar.

With Pup in the remote sit, facing you, raise your right hand at an angle and command "back." Because you raised your right hand, he should spin to his left. If he spins in the wrong direction, whistle the "sit" command and shout a harsh but firm "no." Nick Pup with the momentary button on the collar. Shout "no" again. Give him a moment to consider what he did wrong, then repeat the exercise. It won't be long until he fully understands what you want.

Fit to a "t"

At this point in the training, your dog is completely reinforced in the "t" pattern on land. He can leave your side at home plate and can "line out." He will obey the remote sit, and from there go back to the pile—and farther. He can cast to the right or left—and beyond. He can spin in the proper direction to make a directional back to the right and to the left.

You are now able to direct Pup any place you want. You have mastered the "t" pattern on land. But you're going duck hunting! You need to teach your retriever to take those same directions on water. The "t" pattern on water is called the "swim-by."

● ● ●

10
CHAPTER

The Swim-By

The swim-by teaches Pup to run a blind retrieve in the water by following hand and voice signals. He learns to go back to the pile on second base—and continue back. He learns to come in to you at home plate. He learns to go into a remote sit in the water, looking to you for further instructions. He learns to go over to first base and third base—and beyond. He learns to take a directional back in the water, spinning in the proper direction.

Again, this book teaches how to use the electronic collar to reinforce lessons the dog already knows. Before we move to this new phase of training you must remember one important rule: **Do not use the electronic collar when Pup is in the water**. Yes, like any rule, there are exceptions. But for now, follow the rule without exception.

You are training a water dog, and you want that dog to love the water more than anything. For that reason the dog should rarely feel the sting of the electronic collar while he is in the water, because there is too great a chance you would make Pup afraid to go into the water. I've heard at least one professional trainer express it like this: "The land is hot and the water is cool."

Starting the Swim-By

You're going to start the swim-by the same way you started the "t" pattern—with the force to the pile—but this time you will do it across a body of water. Pup will leave your side on land, dive into the water, swim across the water to a pile of bumpers on the other side of the water, get a bumper in his mouth, and swim back across the water to deliver the bumper to you.

To teach the swim-by you'll need a small body of water with clean banks, if possible a small pond like the one in this photo. Like the "t" pattern on land, a big part of the exercise is repetition; if you try to swim your dog across a large pond time and again, you're going to end up drowning him. And the pond needs to be small enough that you can throw bumpers across it.

For the swim-by, set up a baseball diamond pattern on the edges of a small pond.

Once you've found a pond to use, look for the best place to put home plate and first, second, and third bases. Place a pile of white bumpers at second base. At this point there should be no piles at first and third.

Heel Pup to your side. Make sure he's watching and—just like you did on land—identify the pile by throwing a bumper to it. Since this is a mark, release Pup on the sound of his name. He should dive into the water and retrieve a bumper.

As he is swimming to you with the bumper, you should be standing back some ten feet from the water's edge (more about this in a moment). When Pup comes out of the water and is running to you with the bumper, put him into a remote sit using the whistle command for "sit." At this point he should be sitting in front of you on land, holding the bumper. Take the bumper from him and drop it behind you. It's now time to send the dog "back" to the pile-this time on a blind retrieve for a bumper he did not see thrown.

With Pup at heel, line him up with the pile of bumpers. When he is lined up, command "back." He should leave your side—moving in the direction in which you lined him up—dive into the water, swim across to the pile, and retrieve a bumper from it.

Force to the Pile in Water—with Style

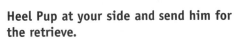

Heel Pup at your side and send him for the retrieve.

As I'm sure you recall, when you forced to the pile on land—after Pup knew what you wanted—you would nick him with the collar every fourth time or so to keep him moving with style and speed. Your new rule of training in water, however, advises you never to use the electronic collar when Pup's in the water. So how do you build style on the swim-by? You nick Pup on the land, before he gets to the water. That's why you are standing at least ten feet back from the water's edge.

To force to the pile, Pup will be standing at your side on land, ten feet from the water. Line him up with the pile and give the "back" command. He will leave your side and run toward the water. Before he hits the water, say "back," nick him with the collar, and repeat "back." Make sure this little "goose" with the collar happens *before* Pup hits the water.

When you're done for the day, throw fun bumpers and praise Pup.

Sending Pup Back from the Remote Sit

There are two ways to send Pup back to the pile. You can line him up at your side, which gives both Pup and you practice in the lining drill. Or you can send him "back" from the remote sit. To do the latter, when he returns from the retrieve with the bumper, whistle him into the remote sit just before he reaches you. Take the bumper, drop it behind you, and give the hand signal and voice command for "back." Pup should spin and go back to the pile. This, of course, reinforces both the spin drill and forcing back to the pile from the remote sit.

Have Pup sit before he reaches you and give the hand signal and voice command "back."

At this point, your dog should be a champ at the remote sit on land. It's time to teach him to do a remote sit in the water.

The Remote Sit in Water

On land the remote sit means that Pup stops, turns to you, and sits while he awaits further instructions. In the water the remote sit means that he stops, turns to you, and treads water as he awaits further instructions. If your dog has been doing well on the remote sit on land, the remote sit in water may come naturally to him. If he does not seem to understand what you want, though, there is a method to teach him.

This training method requires that you attach two long check cords to the dog's collar. One of the check cords will lead back to you. The second leads across the water to your assistant, as shown in the photograph.

To teach this lesson, line Pup up with the pile and send him on a back. He should leave your side, dive into the water, and swim for the pile of bumpers. Both you and your assistant should keep the check cords slightly taut, preparing to use them to stop Pup only if necessary. Keeping the slack out of the line also prevents the dog from becoming entangled in the check cords.

Command "sit" when Pup gets to the crossover. If he doesn't tread water and stay in the same place, you and your partner should pull gently on the cords to make him tread water.

Pup should swim across the water, get a bumper in his mouth, and swim back to you. As he starts back across the pond with the bumper, blow the whistle command for "sit." If he goes into the remote sit, there is no need to use the check cords. If he does not sit, you and your assistant should tighten the check cords at the appropriate point, holding Pup in place, as shown in the photograph. Be careful to tighten the cords gently; don't yank sharply in both directions.

Once he understands the remote sit in water, drill him on it but, as with all lessons, don't overdo it. Do three backs all the way to the pile for every one time you stop him and put him into the remote sit in the water. If you stopped Pup in the same spot every time, you'd create a "popping" problem. Let's look at that.

Popping

Popping occurs when a dog anticipates that you want him to stop at the halfway point to the pile and goes into a remote sit without hearing a command from you. It can happen on land or in water. It's bad for hunting, and it will ruin you in a field trial. Popping is difficult to correct, so it's best to avoid popping in the first place. The best way to prevent popping is to break up the exercise. Send Pup back to the pile on second base three or four times for every time you ask for a remote sit.

Overs in the Water: Step One

Overs in the water are exactly like overs on land. Pup learns to cast over to one side, then to the other side, following the horizontal line in the "t" pattern.

To teach overs in the water, start with Pup on land in the remote sit. Cast him back across the water toward the pile on second base. As he approaches the middle of the pond, blow the "sit" command on the whistle. He should turn to you and tread water, awaiting further instructions. Make sure he is watching, then toss a white bumper over to the first-base area. This is just the spot of you have designated as first base; there is no pile of bumpers there yet.

At this early stage of the lesson, Pup may start to swim for the bumper. Don't let him. "Sit" means "Sit until I release you." If he starts to go for the bumper, blow the whistle command for "sit." When he turns to you, treading water, shout "no." Give Pup a few seconds to realize you were very unhappy with what he did. Then give the hand signal, casting him in the direction you threw the bumper as you command "over." He should leave the remote sit and swim to get the bumper.

As Pup swims to first base, walk around the pond to that location so that you're on shore to greet him when he gets the bumper. Call him out of the water and praise him for a job well done.

Go back to home plate and continue the exercise. Send Pup back to the pile at second base. Don't stop him; just send him straight back. After a few times going straight back to the pile at second, it's time to teach him to cast to third base.

Whistle Pup into a remote sit in the middle of the pond. Make sure he is watching and toss a bumper to third base. Don't let him swim for the bumper until you release him with the hand signal and the "over" command. As he swims to the bumper, walk along the edge of the pond with him. When he gets the bumper in his mouth, call him out of the pond and praise him.

Teaching "overs": With Pup treading water in the middle of the pond, give him the "over" command and signal and send him to retrieve the bumper on third base.

Continue this exercise for another couple of days, alternating overs with forcing back to the pile. A good ratio is to force back to the pile three times for every time you cast to the side.

Overs in the Water: Step Two

The purpose of step two is to keep Pup going back to second base, while teaching him, over and over again, that he cannot go to the piles at first or third bases unless you give him permission. Start by adding piles of white bumpers on the edge of the pond at first and third bases—at the edge because you want this to be as easy for the dog as possible.

With piles now at first, second, and third bases, heel Pup at home plate. Line him up and send him to second base using the command "back." If he veers off course and tries to swim to the pile at first or third, whistle him into the remote sit, shout a harsh "no," and call him back. With Pup at your side, send him back to the pile at second base.

(Note: Some trainers, after stopping the dog with the remote sit, shout "no," nick the dog with the collar, shout "no" again, and call the dog in. This, of course, violates the rule of never using the collar when the dog is in the water. The only argument I can think of in favor of this indirect pressure in the water is that only the nick button, and not the continuous button, is used. If you feel you need to use the nick button in this situation, by all means use it sparingly. Remember, you're running the risk of the dog associating the water with discomfort, and that's not an association you want the dog to make.)

Overs in the Water: Step Three

For the next step of teaching overs, place piles of bumpers at first, second, and third bases. The bumpers at first and third are placed on the pond's edge so that Pup does not have to get all the way out of the water to retrieve them. Heel Pup at home plate and toss a bumper to second base to identify that pile. Use the dog's name to send him to retrieve that mark. When he returns, sit him in the remote sit in front of you. Take the bumper from him and drop it behind you. With Pup watching you and waiting for direction, raise your hand and command "back." He will turn and force back to the pile.

Send him back to the pile at second base three times. After the third try, send him back toward the same pile, but when he is at the halfway point, whistle him into the remote sit. He should stop, tread water, and look to you for direction. When he does, lean out—exaggerating your body language—as you give the hand signal to cast to first base and command "over."

Command "over," sending Pup for the bumper at first base.

Pup should swim to the pile at first base. If he doesn't, identify the pile by throwing a bumper to first base and then command "over." When he casts to get the bumper at first base, walk along the edge of the water, stopping at the corner of the pond. Pup will get the bumper in his mouth and try to get out of the water. Don't let him get out of the water. At this point, it is very important that you start to teach him that he has to stay in the water.

When Pup tries to get out of the water, blow the whistle command for "sit." While he is in the remote sit waiting for further instruc-

Pup may try to get out of the water after making the retrieve, but don't let him leave the water. Blow your sit whistle and command him to stay in the water.

tion, stand at the corner of the pond—in the first-base area on the edge of the water—so that he can clearly see your hand signal. Lean toward third base with exaggerated body language, give the hand signal to third base, and command "over." Pup may want to get out of the water and be with you. You don't want that. He must obey the command to cast back over to the pile on third base.

Do not take no for an answer. If Pup will not get back into the water and cast to the other side on command, be more firm. Mover closer to him and make sure he sees your hand signal. Using very exaggerated body language and a severe tone of voice, command "over."

If he refuses to go back into the water and make the cast, you can nick him with the collar, but there's a way to do it when he is out of the water. It works like this: Wait until Pup has all four feet out of the water. Give the command "over." The moment he does not obey the command, whistle him into the sit position. Say "no" in a harsh tone, nick him with the collar, say "no" again, then lean out, give the hand signal to third base and command "over." At this point, he should go back into the water and make the cast to third.

During this part of the lesson, Pup may want to get out of the pond before reaching the third-base pile. To prevent this, walk along the edge of the pond, continuing to give hand and voice signals for "over." When he reaches the other side, praise him for a job well done.

Walk over toward Pup so he can see your hand signal and command him over to third base.

Continue the exercise. From home plate, send Pup back to second base. Every fourth time, when he is halfway across the pond, whistle him into the remote sit. When he looks to you for instruction, send him over to first base. Follow him along the edge of the pond. Stop him at first base. Before he gets out of the water, send him back over to third base. Reinforce the lesson that "over" means "Go over to the other side on my command and do not, under any circumstances, get out of the water."

You may have to walk the banks a few sessions before he makes the connection, but he'll soon realize that he must follow your "over" command no matter what. At that point, you will be able to command "over" to either side of the pond from your position at home plate.

The goal of the swim-by is simply to teach Pup to take your direction to a bird or bumper he did not see go down. If he could understand English, this whole lesson would take five minutes. You would simply point toward the blind and shout, "I'm pretty sure the duck fell right behind that old log." Pup would say "Thanks," and swim to the log. But he can't understand or speak English, so you have devised a new language—a combination of hand signals and voice commands that direct him back, forward, to the sides, and back at an angle. These proven methods get a dog in the vicinity of a downed bird. It's up to nature, through the power of the dog's nose, to do the rest.

• • •

11
CHAPTER

Reinforcing Honoring

I've already talked about honoring in the chapter on the basics. Honoring is what bird dog people call "backing." If two pointing dogs are hunting and one dog makes the "find," the other dog should stay back and "honor" the other dog's point rather than rushing in to steal the point.

The same type of protocol is important for retrievers. If one dog is given permission to make the retrieve, the second dog should sit, remain steady, and honor that dog's retrieve.

In the chapter on basics, I talked about how to teach a dog to honor. Now, let's talk about how to reinforce that lesson using the electronic collar.

To teach honoring you'll need an assistant and another retriever that's adept at honoring.

Before you begin to reinforce the honor lesson using the electronic collar, Pup must already be trained in how to honor. There must be no doubt in his mind regarding what you expect of him in this drill. Pup must also be thoroughly collar-conditioned. If you proceed immediately from teaching the basics of honoring to reinforcing those lessons with the collar without proper collar-conditioning, Pup is going to unravel on you in a short period of time.

However, if he has been trained in the basics of honoring and collar-conditioned, reinforcing his ability to honor is as easy as reinforcing the "sit" command.

You'll need to recruit another retriever to work with Pup on this lesson—a retriever that is already solid in his ability to honor. Let that dog go with your assistant.

Spread the dogs about thirty feet apart. With both dogs in the sit position—Pup with you and the other retriever with your assistant—toss a bumper to the front.

Let your assistant release his dog on the sound of his dog's name. Your assistant's dog should leave the assistant's side and hurry toward the bumper. If your dog makes any attempt to also make the

If Pup breaks to make the retrieve, command "sit' and hit the continuous button on your transmitter until he stops.

It may take a little practice...

...but Pup will soon learn to be steady and honor the other dog's retrieves.

retrieve, command "sit" and instantly hitting the continuous button on your collar transmitter. Pup should sit immediately. The moment his butt gets back on the ground, release the pressure.

(Note: You should be far enough away from the other retriever so that it doesn't hear the "sit" command. Give the command in a normal voice that is loud enough for Pup to hear, but not loud enough to confuse the other dog.)

It won't take long to reinforce Pup's understanding that he does not make any attempt to retrieve that bumper unless he has permission.

When Pup honors several times in a row, reward him by tossing the bumper and giving him permission to make the retrieve. Soon he will see that, if he obeys, he will get his chance to make the retrieve—and that, for a retriever, is always the greatest reward.

•   •   •

PART THREE

School's Out: Real-World Drills

12
CHAPTER

Confidence Blinds

At this point, your trained retriever is rapidly becoming a top dog. He's been to preschool, received his basic education in school, and had those basics reinforced through the proper use of the electronic collar. Now it's time to get out of school and take your first step into the real world of retrieving. That real world begins with drills. (The drills in this section are shown in detail in the *Top Dog II* video.)

These drills build one lesson upon the other, so they should be taught in the order in which they are presented. But after you and Pup learn them, you can practice them in any order you want. In fact, changing the order helps prevent training sessions from going stale.

These drills will be new territory for Pup and new territory is always frightening—to dogs and humans. As I've said many times before, the purpose of the blind retrieve is to teach your dog to follow your whistle commands and hand signals to find a bird or bumper that he did not see fall. The confidence blind makes it easy for Pup to succeed at this task, building his confidence in the process.

To carry out the first confidence blind, go back to the field and place a pile of white bumpers in a triangle formation. Remember to spread the piles out so Pup won't confuse pile A with pile B.

Place a white bucket behind each pile. You're going to send Pup on a blind retrieve. He will soon learn that wherever he sees a white bucket, he'll find a bumper near it. It helps him succeed at this new task.

Heel Pup to your side. Using the "heel" and "here" commands, line him up with one of the piles. When he is lined up, command "dead bird—back," along with the hand signal that points to the pile, as shown in the photograph. Pup should leave your side and move in the direction in which you lined him up. He should find a bumper. When

Line Pup up with the pile.

you send him back on the next blind retrieve, he should find another bumper. After a few more blind retrieves, his confidence will begin to soar—a sure sign that his abilities are growing.

Command "back" and send him for the confidence blind.

Note: If Pup hesitates, or has problems finding the bumper, shorten the distance to the bucket. If he still has problems, walk him to the area of the bucket until he finds a bumper. You want this exercise to be a winning experience for the dog, no matter what it takes to make that happen.

Continue to send Pup on blind retrieves using the white buckets until you feel he is confident in what he's doing.

The Recurring Blind

Use the same three legs you used in the last drill, but this time remove the buckets.

Heel Pup to your side, line him up with one of the piles, and send him with the command "dead bird—back." He should leave your side and run for the pile. At this point don't worry whether or not he performs perfectly. You just want him to get to a bumper from that pile one way or another. Be patient; if he is having trouble finding a bumper, move closer. It will build his confidence even if he finds the bumper as you are moving along behind him.

We will now introduce a variety of confidence blinds for Pup. They are all important because they create opportunities to reinforce the lesson that he must stay on the blind you send him on, no matter what. But as you complete the exercises that follow, take a moment to repeat the simple blind retrieve without the white bucket we have just learned. It will become an exercise he knows he can succeed at and it will give him confidence to handle new lessons.

The Buddy Blind

The white bucket helped build Pup's confidence by giving him an opportunity to win. For the next exercise, you're going to replace that bucket with an assistant we'll call your "buddy."

Begin the buddy blind with you and Pup facing *away* from the part of the field where your buddy will place a bumper. You don't want

Pup to see where the bumper is placed because you want it to be a blind retrieve. Have your buddy place the bumper within a ten-foot radius of where he or she is standing. Use orange bumpers for this exercise; they are easy for humans to see, but a bit more difficult for a dog to locate (they look black to a dog), making this exercise more challenging.

Heel Pup and line him up with the bumper. Your assistant should be standing near the bumper. Using the command "back," send Pup on a blind retrieve. Run this same blind sev-

Pup learns to find the bumper near your buddy.

As Pup gains confidence, have your buddy plant the bumper farther and farther away.

eral times. Soon Pup will realize that he will find a bumper somewhere near the assistant, just as he learned earlier that the bumper would be near the white bucket.

Once Pup is confident in this first step of the buddy blind, have your assistant plant the bumper farther back while you and Pup are pointed in another direction. When the bumper is placed, line up Pup in that direction and send him on the blind.

Following that retrieve, have your buddy move back twenty-five yards and drop another blind. Send

Pup on that blind retrieve. When he is showing confidence at this level, move the blind back another twenty-five yards. Continue moving back until he is retrieving the blind confidently at one hundred yards.

It Isn't Near the Buddy

For this drill, you're going to send him on a blind, but this time the orange bumper won't be near the buddy. If Pup veers toward the buddy instead of maintaining the line you sent him on, it's his mistake and a new training opportunity. Here's how you do it:

Lay out three piles of bumpers, as in earlier exercises. Line Pup up with pile A and have your assistant stand far enough away from pile A that Pup will not be confused. You want Pup to go to the pile you lined him up with, not to your buddy. With that in mind, it wouldn't help to place the buddy too close to pile A. If Pup makes a mistake, you want him to see clearly that he's making a mistake. If he can't at some point comprehend what he has done wrong, then you can't teach him how to do it right.

If Pup makes a mistake and heads toward your buddy, give the "sit" whistle, command "no," and cast him to pile A with the command "back."

Line Pup up with pile A. On the "back" command he should leave your side and head for the pile. With some luck, he'll go straight to the pile, get a bumper, and return to you.

But if he leaves your side, heads for the pile, and angles off in your buddy's direction, he has made a mistake—and created a training opportunity. In correcting him, you will use the same indirect pressure method you used earlier.

When Pup heads for your buddy, give the whistle command for "sit." He should sit and turn to you for direction. With Pup at his school desk, give him a harsh "no." Then, when that's had a chance to sink in, signal him to the pile you sent him to originally with the command "back." He should turn and cast away from the buddy, back toward the blind retrieve that you sent him on in the first place.

Indirect Pressure—With and Without the Collar

Notice that in the last exercise I did not ask you to use the electronic collar as part of the indirect pressure. Earlier Pup has been reinforced on these exercises using the electronic collar. Now is the time to give him an opportunity to obey the command without using the electronic collar. If he does not obey without the use of the collar, you always have the opportunity to use it because the collar should stay on during every training session.

Here's how to correct Pup in this exercise with indirect pressure if the collar is needed. Have your buddy place the orange bumper in the field and then have him move a distance away from the bumper. This will be a blind retrieve so, obviously, don't let Pup see where the bumper is placed.

With Pup at your side, line him up in the direction you want him to go. Command "back." He should leave your side, moving in the direction in which you sent him. If he veers off toward your buddy, blow the whistle command for "sit." Once your dog is in the sit position, shout a harsh "no," nick him with the collar, and shout "no" again in a harsh voice. Once this has had a moment to sink in, use a hand signal to indicate the direction Pup should turn and command "back," sending him in the direction you sent him originally.

If Pup disobeys the command and continues toward your buddy, continue to correct the problem in the same manner, using the indirect pressure with the collar. Sit the dog. Make sure he is listening to you. Correct him with a harsh "no" and a nick from the collar, give it a moment to sink in, and send him back on the original command. Indirect pressure works the same way. Sometimes it's without the collar. Sometimes it's with the collar.

At this point in the exercise, Pup should be going to the pile, staying on the line you set for him, and ignoring your buddy, who is standing somewhere off the path of the blind. In the next drill, you're going to make the buddy diversion even harder to resist.

The Buddy Shoots

For this drill your assistant needs a gun. A blank pistol, the kind used as a starting pistol at a sporting event, works best. There is no reason to have a gun that really shoots; you just want the noise a gun makes and a blank pistol is safer.

The noise of a pistol shot is a good diversion when Pup is running a blind retrieve.

Have your assistant place a blind bumper in the field and then step far enough away to make the exercise effective, as discussed earlier. Using the command "back," send Pup to the pile. When he is halfway to the pile, have your buddy shoot the blank pistol. The dog will either stay on line to the blind or be drawn by the sound of the shot to your assistant.

If Pup is drawn to the gunner, correct him using the same method of indirect pressure that you used earlier. You can do this either with or without the collar, depending on what you need to make the point.

Don't Get That Mark!

For the next drill, you will send Pup on a blind retrieve while your assistant throws a white bumper that Pup can see, and shoots the blank pistol. During these exercises you're creating diversions that may lead to training opportunities. Seeing the bumper thrown (a mark) creates another irresistible diversion.

The sight of the mark and the noise of the blank pistol create distractions that mimic hunting situations and give you perfect opportunities to train Pup to stay focussed.

Have your assistant place an orange bumper (a blind) away from the spot where he will throw the mark. Once the blind is planted, it's OK to let the dog watch. When your buddy is in place, and you're sure Pup is watching, have your buddy throw a white bumper and shoot the pistol.

With Pup at heel, turn and line him up with the blind that was planted earlier. Using the command "back," send him to make the blind retrieve. Pup will be thinking about that freshly thrown mark, and the temptation of going to fetch that mark will be strong. If he veers away from the blind retrieve and goes to fetch the mark, you have your training opportunity.

Stop him with the "sit" command. You did not tell him to retrieve that mark! You told him to leave your side and go in the direction you lined him up. When he is seated facing you, correct him using indirect pressure, and send him back for the blind.

After Pup correctly retrieves the blind, let him retrieve the mark. Remember, the command to retrieve the mark is the dog's name.

The Diversion of a Real Bird

A real bird, even a dead one, is the most tempting diversion of all. If your dog sees a real dead bird thrown and is still able to run the blind you asked him to run without going off course to the real bird, you're on path to creating a top dog.

To do this drill have your assistant plant an orange bumper in the field while Pup is not looking (a blind) and then have the assistant move a fair distance away from that blind. Now direct your dog's attention to the assistant, and while Pup is watching have the assistant shake a dead duck. (If don't have a dead duck handy, you can use a scented duck dummy.)

In any event, shake the dead duck or the scented dummy. Let Pup get crazy for retrieving that duck, and then signal your assistant to throw the duck high into the air and shoot the pistol. Pup should be standing by your side, eagerly awaiting the command to retrieve the duck. Say the dog's name (which is always the command to pick up a mark) and he should show little hesitation in heading out to pick up the duck.

At this point it's time to turn, line Pup up, and send him on the blind that was placed earlier. The diversion will be the scent of the dead duck from the earlier mark. If he veers off the line of the blind and heads toward the scent of the dead duck, give him the "sit" command, correct him using indirect pressure, and send him back on the blind that you sent him on originally. Pup must learn that he must do what you ask him to do every time.

Stay with each level of these exercises until Pup does it

Have your buddy throw the dead duck and shoot the blank pistol.

If Pup heads away from the blind and toward the scent of the dead duck, give the "sit" command, correct him with indirect pressure, and send him to the hidden bumper.

right every time. You may stay on one level of the exercise for several training sessions, but that's OK. Staying with each step of the exercise over a period of time gives you the opportunity for the basis of good training—consistency and repetition.

Always remember to build Pup's self-assurance by running the simple confidence blind at least once during each training session. Finding the bumper every time gives him confidence for the other lessons.

Now it's time to increase the difficulty of the exercise by going to the cold blind.

• • •

13
CHAPTER

The Cold Blind

In a cold blind the dog is asked to make a blind retrieve in a situation where he saw nothing happen whatsoever. Suppose you and your dog arrive at the blind in your boat. Your hunting partner has been waiting for you, and he tells you excitedly that he downed a mallard five minutes earlier. He knows the general area where the duck went down and wants your retriever to make the blind retrieve. This is a cold blind because the dog has no idea where that bird might be. He is completely dependent upon your commands and hand signals to get into the area of the downed duck.

To carry out this drill, you will start on land. Plant an orange bumper, making sure, since it's a blind, that Pup is not watching. When you plant the bumper, tie a ribbon to a nearby bush or tree limb, or plant a "blind pole," an orange stick about four feet long, as shown in the photo. The ribbon or the blind pole is there simply to help you remember where the bumper is hidden. Any device or similar reminder will work just fine as long as it is not so obvious that it serves

A blind pole will help you remember where the bumper is hidden.

the same purpose the white bucket served in the early step of the confidence blind.

The difference between the confidence blind and the cold blind is that the confidence blind was run using the three piles of white bumpers spread out like bases on a baseball field. The cold blind uses one lone orange bumper hidden anywhere, and the dog has no clue about its location. He will have to trust you to guide him there.

Line Pup up with the bumper. Get him leaning forward, then command "back." He should leave your side and run in the direction in which you lined him up. There are no diversions. You simply want Pup to find the bumper and bring it to you. Once he does, praise him and put him away for the day.

In the cold blind, Pup will have no idea where the bumper is and will have to trust you to guide him to it.

It's a good idea to intersperse the cold blind with the confidence blinds. You are building Pup's confidence in knowing that he will find a bumper when he moves in the direction in which you send him. If you have to place the bumper closer for Pup to be successful, do it. Success builds confidence.

As he gets better at it, you can increase the distance of the planted bumper, up to about twenty yards. After Pup starts finding bumpers

Success builds confidence.

twenty yards away, he will begin to think that you just might know a thing or two about where he can find something to retrieve. That's what you want—Pup gaining confidence in himself, and in you.

• • •

14

The Wagon Wheel

Notice that all of these blind drills require that Pup leave your side, move in the direction in which you lined him up, and stay on that line until further instruction. In order to reinforce his ability to stay on that tight line, we use a drill called the wagon wheel.

Basically the drill is simple. You and Pup stand in the hub of the wheel, and you send him out to retrieve on several lines from that hub—like the spokes of a wagon wheel.

Lining a dog up for a blind retrieve means that he is to move in the exact direction you've indicated until he finds the blind or until you give him additional instructions. It also means that Pup must come straight back to you on the same line he went out on. The wagon wheel drill reinforces his ability to stay on that tight line out and back.

In the wagon wheel, you teach Pup to stay on a tight line by teaching him to "thread the needle" between two white bumpers on his way to retrieve a more distant orange bumper.

To prepare for the wagon wheel, place eight white bumpers in a circle, or a "wheel," as shown in the diagram on the next page. In the early stages of the exercise, the white bumpers that form the wheel should be about fifteen feet from the center and about eight feet apart. Eventually the space between the white bumpers (the "eye" of the needle) will narrow, but for now you want to make it easy for Pup to succeed.

Place an orange bumper between each set of white bumpers, but about fifteen feet beyond the white bumpers. When the set-up is complete, there should be eight white bumpers along the outside of the wheel and eight orange bumpers out beyond the wheel. Pup is color blind, so the orange bumpers will look black to him. This makes them a bit harder for him to see—adding to the challenge—and it distinguishes them from the white bumpers, which will be important.

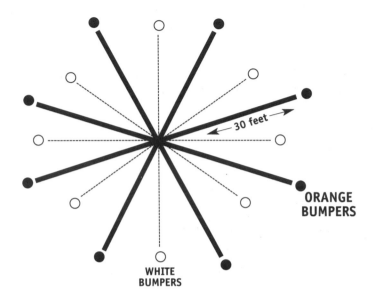

30 feet

ORANGE BUMPERS

WHITE BUMPERS

The wagon wheel. The white bumpers should be placed 15 feet from the center of the wheel; the orange between each white bumper and 15 feet farther out.

The object of the drill is for Pup to leave your side and stay on a tight, straight line to one of the orange bumpers in the distance and then return on the same line.

This is how the wagon wheel will actually look. Note: You and Pup stand at the center of the wheel.

You're ready to begin the exercise. Bring Pup into the center of the wheel. Heel him and line him up with one of the orange bumpers. He did not see the orange bumper thrown, so it's a blind. Give the command "back." If Pup is lined up properly, he should leave your side, thread right between the two white bumpers, and retrieve the orange bumper. If he tries to get off line or to pick up a white bumper, sit him, correct him using indirect pressure, and call him back. Heel him to your side, line him up, and send him again.

When Pup gets it right, praise him and continue the exercise. You do not have to go around the circle in any certain order. Line Pup up at random with any orange bumper and run the exercise.

Wagon Wheel: Step Two

When Pup is retrieving with confidence, it's time to make the drill a little more difficult. To do that, simply move the white bumpers a little closer together, forcing Pup to stay on a tighter line. Also move the orange bumpers farther out. You'll need twelve white bumpers and twelve orange bumpers for this tighter circle.

If Pup goes off line to pick up a white bumper, make him sit and correct him with the collar.

Bring Pup back to the center of this new, tighter circle. Heel him and line him up with any one of the orange bumpers and send him on a blind using the "back" command. If he gets off line, stop him immediately by putting him into the remote sit, correct him with indirect pressure, and call him in. With Pup at your side, line him up again with the same bumper and make him try it again.

Continue this wagon wheel over and over, slowly making the space between the white bumpers more and more narrow while placing the orange bumpers farther and farther away. Use your own common sense about how narrow is too narrow. You want the dog to keep building on winning situations.

As Pup advances in the wagon wheel drill, the white bumpers are placed closer together and the orange ones farther out to make the training more challenging.

Once Pup is confident on the wagon wheel, he should have a solid understanding of going straight out and coming straight back. One situation that can cause a dog to get off the straight line is "bank cheating." The drill that is designed to prevent "cheating the banks" is called the cheating single.

• • •

15
CHAPTER

The Cheating Single

Cheating the banks simply means that instead of Pup jumping into the water and swimming straight to a downed bird, he runs around the banks to reach the bird. At some point every dog will try to run the banks for one simple reason: It's easier. And dogs, like humans, have been known to take the easy way out on occasion.

Even though this approach might seem logical to the dog, it is unacceptable in a hunting situation. Cheating the banks can be dangerous. If a dog does this in a swamp area, for example, he could get lost or fall prey to some other danger like quicksand. He could also end up trespassing on land where you don't have permission to hunt. In field trials, cheating the banks will immediately take your dog out of the competition. A retriever has to go straight to the downed bird and straight back. Running the banks, as it is sometimes also called, is never acceptable.

Pick a pond that is shaped like a channel—long and thin. This gives you a chance to plant a bumper near the bank while forcing the dog to swim next to the bank for a long distance. The urge to get out of the water and cheat the banks will be strong.

To run the cheating single drill, place an assistant with white bumpers beside the pond. Heel Pup and give him the "mark" command. He should know by now that this means something is about to happen, and he should look to the front. When he does, have the assistant wave the bumper and toss it into the water a couple of feet from the bank he's standing on. As he tosses the bumper, have him shoot a blank pistol. This is a mark, so give Pup permission to make the retrieve on the sound of his name. He should dive into the water and swim straight to the bumper and straight back.

For most retrievers, it doesn't usually happen quite so neatly on the first several attempts. Most don't even attempt to get in the water.

Given the command to retrieve, they run toward the water, but as soon as they reach the water's edge, they cheat the bank until they are just across from the bumper and then they enter the water.

If this happens with Pup, you can handle this training opportunity by using indirect pressure and the electronic collar when he is not in the water. But, the first few times, try to handle it without the use of the collar like this:

Give the command for Pup to retrieve the mark. He runs toward the water, but then veers off and runs the bank, heading toward the mark. The moment he commits to cheat the bank, blow the whistle command for "sit." Pup should turn toward you and sit. Shout a harsh "no," give it a moment to sink in, call him to you, and start the process again. Give this approach several chances to work without the use of the electronic collar.

When Pup cheats and attempts to run around the pond to retrieve the bumper, give him the "sit" whistle...

If Pup persists in cheating the banks, use indirect pressure and the electronic collar—the same indirect pressure you have always used.

Have your assistant throw the bumper and shoot the gun. Give the command to retrieve the mark. Pup will leave your side. The moment he commits to cheat the bank, blow the whistle command for "sit." When he gives you his attention, shout a harsh "no," nick him with the collar, shout "no" again and let it sink in, call him in, and start the whole process again.

Another way to handle the same problem is to use indirect pressure with the collar, but instead of calling Pup in and starting over, cast him back to the mark. It works like this:

Now cast Pup over into the water...

When Pup makes the mistake of cheating the bank, give the "sit" command. Shout "no." Correct him with the collar. Shout "no" again. Then cast him back into the water and toward the bumper, using the hand signal and the command "over." He should swim to the mark.

If he wants to get out of the water and cheat the bank at this point, you have a different situation. Remember, you never use the electronic collar when a dog is in the water. How, then, do you correct Pup if he commits to make the mistake of getting out of the water to cheat the banks? There is a plan. It goes like this:

And then back toward the bumper.

Pup is swimming along the edge of the bank. The mark is way ahead. He sees an easier way—getting out and running along the bank. He swims toward the bank, clearly making an effort to get out of the water.

Pup should also swim straight back to you on the return trip.

Your first option is to put him in a remote sit, bark a harsh "no," and—using hand signals and voice commands—cast him back to the mark. If that indirect pressure without the electronic collar works, you're fine.

If you have to use the collar, wait until Pup has all four feet out of the water. The moment all four feet are on the land, sit him with the whistle, bark your harsh "no," correct him with the nick of the electronic collar, and cast him back into the water to the mark.

If you've built your dog's training one basic block at a time, and if those basics have been reinforced, Pup will soon get the idea that he has to stay in the water all the way out to the bumper and all the way back. When he does it right, praise him.

If Pup cannot get this behavior right, though, there is another drill that reinforces the behavior of swimming straight out and straight back. It's called channel marks.

• • •

16
CHAPTER

Channel Marks and Channel Blinds

Channel marks are simple. They're just a row of bumpers tossed out into a long narrow pond or channel.

To carry out the channel mark drill, have your assistant throw four (or more) white bumpers in a line down the middle of the channel. (If you don't have access to a long, thin pond, you can apply the same principle on other waters. The goal is to get a line of bumpers floating, one after another, in an area where the dog will be tempted to get out of the water and cheat the banks.)

Let Pup watch the assistant tossing the bumpers. You want these to be marks. Give him the "mark" command and, using his name to release him, send him on a retrieve. He should dive eagerly into the water, get the first bumper in the line, and return it to you. Once he has done that, drop the bumper

Channel marks are simply a way of building Pup's confidence in water retrieves.

behind you and send him for the next mark (they're all marks, since he saw them all fall).

In this drill all you're doing is building Pup's confidence that he can stay in the water all the way out to the bumper and all the way back.

After you have done this drill for a while, use a single mark — a large white bumper so Pup can see it easily — at the end of the channel. If he tries to cheat the bank, correct him with indirect pressure, as described earlier. If he successfully completes the drill, praise him, throw fun bumpers, and put him away for the day.

Once Pup can do the channel mark over and over again, it's time to go to the channel blind.

The Channel Blind

To carry out the channel blind drill, use the same long narrow pond.

Have your assistant place an orange bumper at the end of the channel. This is a blind, so don't let Pup see the bumper being placed. Since the dog has not seen a bumper thrown or heard a gun shot, this will be a cold channel blind. Pup will have no idea there is something out there for him to retrieve until you line him up and send him. But, by now, he's gaining confidence in himself and in you. If the boss says there's something out there, he is coming to believe it and he'll look forward enthusiastically to retrieving it.

On the "back" command, Pup should leave your side, moving in the direction that you lined him up. He should swim straight on that line, and when he reaches the end of the channel, he should find the bumper and swim straight back to you. That's the way it's supposed to work.

On either the way out or on the way back, however, Pup could see the easier way and try to cheat the banks. When he does, you have to stop him and correct him, using the methods of indirect pressure. As soon as he commits to make the mistake, stop him, shout "no," and cast him back or call him in, depending upon whether he has the bumper or not.

If indirect pressure without the electronic collar does not work, wait until he has all four feet out of the water and correct him with indirect pressure using the electronic collar. Following the correction, cast him back to the bumper if he has not yet made the retrieve.

If Pup has already picked up the bumper, however, you can't simply call him in. He could easily think that means you want him to run back to you on the bank, which is exactly what you don't want. You want him to go back into the water and swim to you. To get that behavior, first—after correcting Pup—cast him back into the water. Once he is in the water, put him in a remote sit with the whistle. Now he is treading water looking to you for further instruction, and you can call him in using the whistle command for "here."

• • •

17
CHAPTER

Reentry

As you know, when making a retrieve in water, Pup should swim straight out to the downed bird, make the retrieve, and swim straight back. Sometimes in the real world, however, to stay on a straight line, Pup will have to get out of the water, cross a small piece of land, and get back into another body of water to continue toward the bird. Getting out of the water, crossing the land, and getting back into the water is called the reentry.

To carry out this exercise, you'll need a body of water separated by a piece of land. This could be a peninsula that juts out into a pond, or it might be the small piece of land between two separate ponds. Any area will work where the dog has to get out of the water, cross a small piece of land, and get back into the water, as shown in the diagram.

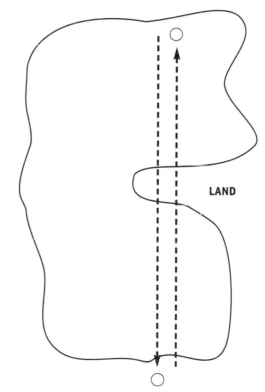

To practice reentries, find a body of water separated by a piece of land.

LAND

To teach reentry, you start with a simple retrieve. Stand on the strip of land that separates the two bodies of water. Toss a white bumper into the second (more distant) water. When Pup has accomplished this simple retrieve, move to the far side of the first body of water, as shown in the diagram. Heel Pup to your side. When you're sure he is watching, have your assistant toss a white bumper into the second body of water. In order to make the retrieve, Pup will have to swim across the first body of water, get out of the water, cross the land, and get back into the water. If he does this without further encouragement, he understands reentry. If he doesn't make the retrieve, go back to the land that separates the two bodies of water and start over. When Pup makes that retrieve, move back and repeat the reentry exercise. Eventually he will make the connection and understand that it's OK to get out of the water and cross the spit of land to make the retrieve.

There is a potential problem with reentry that I want you to be aware of. You can create a reentry problem if you nick Pup too many times in the earlier drills to prevent him from getting out of the water to cheat the banks. The connection is logical. If every time the dog tried to get out of the water to cheat the banks, you nicked him, it could make him nervous about getting out of the water for reentry. That's just one more reason not to use the electronic collar when the dog is in the water. If you have to use the electronic collar to prevent bank cheating, don't use it until the dog has all four feet out of the water. Still, if the dog is nicked too many times just as he gets his feet on land, he may become reticent about getting out of the water. It is easier to prevent this problem than to cure it. You do that by being very sparing in your use of the electronic collar when the dog is in or near the water.

• • •

18
CHAPTER

The Tune-Up Drill

In making a retrieve, Pup should go straight out, get the bumper or the bird, and come straight back. It's also important that he enter the water at the correct angle to stay on that straight line.

Let's say that in order to make a retrieve on a straight line out, the dog must enter the water at a 45-degree angle, as shown in the illustration. When they reach the water's edge, however, many dogs have a natural tendency to slow down and square their shoulders with the

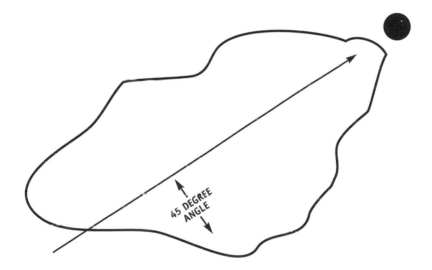

45 DEGREE ANGLE

Pup must learn to enter the water on an angle—not perpendicular to the shore—to stay on a straight line while making a retrieve.

shore before entering the water. You want your dog to enter the water on the same line and angle to the water he established on land. In this drill you'll give him practice on entering the water at an angle.

Place a blind so that, in order to stay on a straight line out to the blind, Pup will have to enter the water at an angle. Line him up with the blind and send him using the command "back." He should leave your side, moving in the direction in which you lined him up. When Pup gets to the water, he should stay on that straight line and enter the water at an angle. If he does, great! If he does not, correct the problem, using indirect pressure:

The blind is placed so that Pup must enter the water at a 45 degree angle to correctly make the retrieve.

1. Call him back to you and send Pup from your side toward the blind. When he slows down and begins to square his shoulders with the water's edge, stop him with the "sit" whistle **before he enters the water.**

2. With Pup in the sit position listening to you, shout a harsh "no" and give it a second to sink in, then cast him back using hand signals and the command "back." Pup should turn and enter the water at an angle. (Move in closer to make the hand signals very clear if you need to. Hand signals allow Pup to see the angle you want.)

    If Pup stops to square up with the water again, sit him again with the whistle and correct him once more using indirect pressure. If you have to add the nick of the collar to the indirect pressure, then do so. But only use the collar if the dog is still on the bank and not yet in the water.

    When your dog is succeeding at entering the water at an angle, run the exercise on five different blinds from five different angles around the pond, as shown in the illustration. When Pup can successfully enter

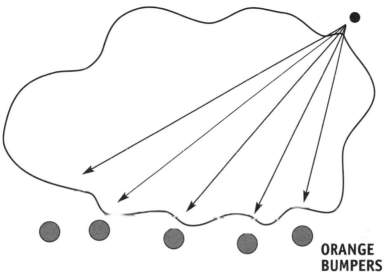

**ORANGE
BUMPERS**

**Five bumpers, five different practice angles. To stay on a straight line
to the bumpers, Pup must enter the water at five different angles.**

the water at those five different angles, you know he's catching on. And,
when he gives you want you want, praise him a whole bunch.

If he slows down during this exercise, give him with a nick
from the collar *before* he enters the water.

Holding a Tight Line

For the next step, you will give Pup practice on holding a tight line to
the bumper and back. You're going to ask him to maintain that tight
line all the way to the end of the channel and back, swimming just
about four to five feet from the bank. This gives you the opportunity to
reinforce two behaviors — staying on a tight line and refusing the strong
temptation to get out of the water and cheat the banks.

Place the blind at the end of the channel and approximately four
feet from the bank. At the other end of the channel, heel Pup to your
side. Both you and he should also be about four feet from the side of
the channel.

Line Pup with the blind and send him to make the retrieve using the command "back." He should enter the water and swim in a straight line toward the blind.

Watch Pup closely for any sign that he's starting to pull toward the bank. If he moves toward the bank, stop him immediately with the "sit" whistle. He should turn toward you, treading water and waiting for further instruction. Shout "no," give that a moment to sink in, and cast him back toward the blind with voice and a hand signal.

It's important that you be quick with these commands. Don't wait until he is three feet off the line before you correct him. The moment you see Pup commit to make the mistake, stop him with the whistle. When he is turned toward you, cast him back toward the blind.

Retrieves close to the bank will increase Pup's ability to hold a tight line on the way out and on the way back.

Hitting the Water with Speed and Style

By now Pup is entering the water at an angle. If he doesn't slow down at water's edge, he's doing everything right. If he does slow down, the tune-up drill gives you an opportunity to correct that. Use the same method you used earlier to nick the dog on his way to the pile. This nick is the invisible crop that says, "Get going and keep moving. I want hustle!" Line Pup up at least fifteen feet from the water and send him to the blind on the command "back." While he is still on land, running toward the water, nick him to urge him along. He should be familiar with this experience from his earlier training on force to the pile, and he should hit the water with speed and style.

•   •   •

19
CHAPTER

The Lining Drill

When making a retrieve, the top dog leaves your side, swims straight to the downed bird, makes the retrieve, and swims straight back to you. It is important that the dog stay on a straight line out and back—even if he encounters obstacles. In the world of retrievers, an obstacle is called a "concept."

Obstacles can be anything in the dog's path—a downed tree, a small island, or a spit of land. Unless the dog is directed to go around the concept, the dog is expected to stay on line. As always, you want to use your common sense. I've never met a trainer who wanted his dog to go over rather than around a beaver dam. The ends of those beaver-dam sticks are sharp and can kill a dog. Be reasonable. Send the dog around an obstacle like that.

Unless directed to go around it, Pup should stay on a line and go over, under, or through any obstacle.

But there are obstacles that it is reasonable to have a dog go over or through. Here's how to teach him to stay on a straight line through the concept.

In setting up this drill, use anything that will create an obstacle between the dog and a pile of bumpers. For example, you can make a concept using a bench, an old lawn chair, or by laying a plank across two concrete blocks.

Create a pile of white bumpers and place the concept between Pup and the pile of bumpers. While he is watching, identify the pile by throwing a bumper to it, making it a mark. Release Pup on the sound of his name. He should leave your side to make the retrieve, staying on line over, under, or through the obstacle and returning the same way. If he will do that, give him plenty of praise, run the drill a few times, and call it very good day of training.

The desire to go around an obstacle is almost always greater than the desire to go over it. That's where training comes in.

If Pup tries to go around the obstacle, however, correct the problem using indirect pressure. Line him up and send him to the pile. When he tries to go around the concept, put him in a remote sit with the whistle. Shout, "no!" in a harsh tone, let it sink in, call him in, and start again.

If indirect pressure without the collar does not work, use the collar. Send Pup to the pile. When he starts to make the mistake, sit him with the whistle, shout "no" in an unhappy tone, nick him with the collar, and shout "no" again. Let it sink in, call him back, and try again. Soon he will get the idea that what he is doing is wrong. Be quick with that whistle so he can understand the behavior you want him to change.

If Pup refuses to go over the concept, move closer to it and try again. If he continues to try to go around the concept, keep moving closer until he has no choice but to go over it. Once he's going over it, move back gradually, until you can send him from twenty-five yards back and he will still go over, rather than around, the obstacle.

Pup must come in the same way he went out—over the obstacle.

That is how you correct the problem using indirect pressure if Pup is going out to make the retrieve. But what if he has picked up the bumper and tries to go around the obstacle on the way in? How do you correct that problem? You correct that problem through the use of attrition.

Attrition

According to *Webster's New World Dictionary*, "attrition" means "the act of weakening or exhausting by constant harassment or abuse." You certainly don't want to harass or abuse your dog, but that's the label that was put on this drill, and to some extent it helps if you stay with a common set of words used by many retriever trainers.

Attrition is an exercise often used with a headstrong dog that won't listen to you. If your retriever is running wild, doing things his way, you can wear him down with whistle commands and hand signals. Use the whistle to bring him in, send him back, send him over, and then bring him in again until he is grateful to listen to you and do it your way.

Let's talk about how to use attrition to correct a dog when he avoids an obstacle on his way back from the pile.

Let's assume the obstacle, or concept, you have set up for this drill is a picnic bench tipped over on its side. Pup goes over the bench to make the retrieve, gets the bumper from the pile, and as he is coming back toward you he veers off line to go around the bench. The moment he begins to make the mistake, sit him with the whistle. Shout a harsh "no," nick him with the collar, then shout "no" again. Give Pup a moment to think about what just happened, and cast him back to let him have another chance to come in straight to you. If you called him in to you after the indirect pressure, you'd be telling him that going around the obstacle and coming to you was what you wanted. That is not what you want.

Once Pup is back and the bench is between you and him, sit him, then call him in to you. If he makes a straight line over the obstacle to you, praise him.

But, if he tries to go around the obstacle again, start over with the attrition process. Sit him. Correct him. Cast him back, and then call him in. When Pup is cast back and called in often enough, he'll finally wear down and do it the right way. That's why they call it attrition. When he gets it right, praise him for the proper behavior, throw fun bumpers, and end the training for the day.

You can use attrition anytime Pup is acting headstrong in the field. Attrition simply means you can bring Pup in, cast him back, cast him over, and bring him in until he realizes that he is not running the show. You are. Use the electronic collar during the attrition process only if Pup insists on doing things his way.

Although the electronic collar is not required in the attrition exercise per se, there is always the possible need for the collar to enforce the basics. If you blew the whistle command for "sit," for example, and Pup refused to obey, you could use the collar to enforce "sit." The attrition drill is based on the basics of "sit," "here," "back," and "over."

- - •

20
CHAPTER

The Poison Bird

Imagine that while hunting you knock down two ducks. The first duck falls in the distance and you don't see clearly where it landed. You think it might be behind some trees and it appears to be wounded. The second duck falls in front of you with a big splash that both you and Pup see clearly. The first duck is a blind. The second duck is a mark.

You want Pup to retrieve the wounded duck in the distance first, before it has time to move to another location. But Pup wants to retrieve that marked bird that landed right in front of him in the worst way. You know that duck isn't going anywhere, so you tell him "no" while he stares at the bird in front of him, line him up with the blind in the distance, and send him to make the blind retrieve.

If Pup insists on ignoring your efforts to retrieve the blind first and retrieves the marked bird first, he has retrieved a "poison bird." A poison bird can kill your dog's chances of winning a field trial. And it can make your hunting much more difficult.

In this exercise you will learn how to teach Pup to make the retrieve you ask him to make, even though the desire to retrieve the mark he just saw fall may be extremely strong. The poison bird drill is carried out in the following manner:

When Pup is not watching, hide an orange bumper at the end of the pond. That bumper will be your blind retrieve. Heel Pup to you. When you're sure he is watching, toss a second bumper into the water in front of you and the dog. So as not to confuse Pup, toss the mark a fair distance away from the path of your blind retrieve.

Pup will be watching the mark wanting to retrieve it in the worst way. Heel him around to you using the "here" and "heel" commands. Line him up with the blind at the end of the pond and give the "back" command that releases him to make a blind retrieve. Pup should leave your side, hit the water, and swim toward the blind as directed.

Pup is tempted by the mark ("poison bird"). As in hunting situations, Pup must learn to ignore the close bird and go after the blind as directed.

If he veers off that line and starts for the mark, he has made a mistake. You correct this mistake, using the same indirect pressure you have been using in earlier training situations.

The moment Pup veers off the line to swim toward the mark, stop him with the "sit" whistle. When he turns and gives you his attention, shout a harsh "no." Then, using hand and voice signals, cast him back toward the blind. If he obeys and moves toward the blind, congratulations are in order for both you and Pup. He's completed a successful drill. If Pup does not obey and continues toward the mark, stop him again with the whistle and repeat the process.

Give this approach every opportunity to work without the use of the electronic collar because the dog is in the water. But if you have tried repeatedly and you're certain that Pup knows what you want but is just ignoring you, you may, sparingly, use the nick button on the collar. Use it the same way you've always used it with indirect pressure.

Line Pup up and send him on the blind retrieve. The moment he veers off course and commits to swim to the mark, stop him with the "sit" whistle. When he stops and gives you his attention, shout a harsh "no" and nick him with the collar. Follow that by shouting a second harsh "no," give him a moment to realize what he just did and associate it with the harsh "no," and use hand and voice signals to cast him back toward the blind at the end of the pond.

• • •

21
CHAPTER

The Diversion Bird

The diversion bird is one that can divert your dog away from his original mission. A top dog must stay on his mission unless given permission to do otherwise. This drill will reinforce the behaviors that teach your dog to not be led astray by a diversion bird.

Picture yourself hunting with a partner when two mallards come in. Your partner gets one. You send your dog to make the retrieve. He swims out and gets the duck. When he is returning, another mallard flies toward your duck blind. It spreads its wings over your decoys and you nail it.

Pup is swimming back in with the first retrieve; that is the mission you sent him on. He needs to stay on that mission. If, however, on his way back he sees the second duck fall and tries to retrieve it, that is a "diversion" bird.

It is important that Pup complete the original retrieve first, then—with your permission—return to make the second retrieve. To reinforce Pup's ability to ignore the diversion bird, create a training opportunity.

Plant a blind bumper at the end of the pond. Line up Pup and send him on the blind

When Pup is returning with the blind, toss another bumper just off his path.

retrieve. When he is returning with the blind bumper, toss out another bumper, just off his path.

If he tries to retrieve this diversion bird before completing the first retrieve, correct that behavior using the old standby—indirect pressure. When Pup commits to move toward the diversion bird, stop him with the "sit" whistle. Shout a harsh "no" and call him to you using the voice command or the whistle command for "here." Make him come to you.

After Pup has successfully completed the first retrieve, send him for the diversion bird. Repeat this drill and he will learn that eventually he'll be allowed to make both retrieves. He just needs to do first things first.

I don't feel you should use a nick from the electronic collar in this drill. It would only confuse him. He's making a blind retrieve. If he's nicked for going toward the diversion bird, there is too great a chance that he could confuse that nick with something he's doing right with the blind retrieve.

If Pup tries to retrieve the diversion bird, simply stop him with the whistle, shout a harsh and unhappy "no," and call him in to complete his original mission.

• • •

22
CHAPTER

Training for Upland Game

Many hunters today are using their retrievers for double duty — to retrieve waterfowl and hunt upland game birds.

I must admit, coming from the South and growing up hunting quail behind pointers and setters, for most of my life I'd never seen a retriever hunt upland birds. I took a trip to Montana one fall. It was the opening day of pheasant season. I remarked to a friend that I'd grown up reading Montana pheasant tales in *Field & Stream* magazine, and that it was too bad he didn't have a bird dog so that we could give those pheasants a try. When my friend told me I could take his Labrador retriever, I frankly didn't know what he was talking about. I knew that his Lab could make the retrieve once I'd shot a pheasant, but I needed a dog to find that pheasant. He told me his dog would find the pheasants all right, adding that she'd even stop and hold still long enough to let you know where the pheasant was hiding. That was good enough for me.

We went out to a field near Flathead Lake. The Lab danced out of the truck and began to crisscross the field. It wasn't long before she was standing still, looking a little wide-eyed like she'd found something. I walked in with my gun ready just as a much-noisier-than-I-had-expected rooster exploded into the air, moving faster than I thought they could move. I missed that rooster by a mile, three times! But I came away impressed with the Lab's ability to hunt upland game.

Hunting upland game with a retriever is gaining in popularity — and for good reason. A lot of families only have room for one dog. A well-bred and well-trained retriever can be the perfect family pet while also hunting upland game and waterfowl. A trifecta.

Upland training should begin when your dog is about twelve months old. To start, you go right back to the same basics you have always used. Teaching those basics and reinforcing them are the key to this training.

First, a retriever that bred from parents who were hunters is likely to have a good nose. If he doesn't, he's not going to be able to locate the upland game. If your dog is able to get in the vicinity of a blind retrieve on a real duck and find that blind using his nose, his nose should be plenty good for upland birds.

In addition, most retrievers are smart. It doesn't take a good retriever long to figure out what you want. And, if you've bonded with him properly, he'll be eager to please.

When teaching your retriever to hunt upland game birds, you're simply reinforcing two commands Pup already knows: "over" and "sit."

Bird dogs like setters and pointers are born with "bird sense" in the same way Labs are born with the instinct to retrieve. A bird dog with good bird sense should know more about where the birds are than the human who is bringing up the rear. A bird dog owner knows how to respect and channel this instinct.

But most retrievers are not born with that kind of bird sense. They're smart dogs and they may quickly come to identify places where birds are likely to be, but you don't want the upland retriever to

Smart and versatile, many retrievers perform double duty as upland game dogs.

run wherever he wants to run. You want to teach the retriever to stay out in front of you and to quarter the field. You teach that behavior using the command "over."

Get Pup out in the field. It should be an open field away from dangerous highways and distractions. Pup should be the only dog on the ground; another dog would only be a distraction. You can hunt two dogs in the future, but during these training stages, work with one dog.

Walk briskly into the field and command "hunt 'em up" in an upbeat manner. Tone of voice is important. A positive tone will make Pup feel he has the right to run around looking for something. He will do just that.

Walk around with Pup. Keep him happy; this should be fun. The first lesson you want to get into Pup's head—before he ever sees an upland bird—is that you want him to hunt to your front. To teach that in the beginning stages, simply keep Pup to your front by staying behind him.

Walk through the field. If he moves to your right, turn and move behind him. If he moves to your rear, turn and get behind him. Pup should soon get the idea that he is supposed to stay in front.

Once he is working consistently in front of you, you need to teach him to zigzag, or quarter, across the

Keep Pup in front of you by using "over" commands.

field. That way he will cover more territory and find more birds. Use the "over" command to teach Pup to quarter a field. When he is working to your front, whistle the "sit" command to get his attention. When he's looking to you for direction, lean out using exaggerated body language and command "over." He should begin to hunt in the direction you cast him. Walk forward, and if you want, add the command "hunt 'em up!" to urge him forward.

When you're ready for your dog to quarter in the other direction, whistle to get his attention, give a hand signal for the other direction, and command "over." Continue this exercise across the field. Pup will soon get the idea that after he moves to one side of the field, you want him to turn and hunt back to the other side. As long as you are moving forward, Pup will be moving forward into new territory each time he quarters.

The next step is to add an upland bird to the equation. You're not going to teach Pup to point the bird—not like the pointing breeds. Although there are "pointing" retrievers, that's not our focus here. You are going to teach Pup to "stop to flush." When he finds game, you want him to flush the bird and sit so he can mark where the bird goes down. You teach that using the whistle command for "sit." You don't want him to chase the bird after the flush, because then he can't see where the bird went as well, and chasing could be dangerous if he gets in the way of a shot, particularly when more than one bird is flushed from a single location.

A bird launcher hidden in the field will allow you to spring a live bird directly into the air, simulating a real flush.

Most of us don't live where there are enough upland birds for training purposes. Professional bird dog trainers, however, should be able to lead you to someone in your area who raises pen-raised game birds. If not, you can order pen-raised birds advertised in the sporting periodicals. But the truth is that regular ol' barnyard pigeons work just as well. You can trap pigeons at your local feed store. They're abundant and free. They also are strong fliers and they're hearty. In my experience, a bird dog will point a pigeon as quickly as he'll point a bobwhite quail.

Begin this part of the training with a bird launcher. The bird launcher is a sling-like contraption that holds the bird until your ready for the bird to fly. The launcher puts you in control of the training situation. A live bird is put in a spring-loaded harness and when you release the spring—either electronically or with a pull cord—the bird is thrown in the air. This throws the bird up and away from the dog in a hurry so that the dog can't catch it.

Place the bird in the launcher downwind of the dog—that is, with the wind blowing from the dog toward the bird. When you hunt, it's best to point Pup into the wind so the scent of the game drifts down to him (the birds would be upwind). But at this point in the training you're not teaching Pup to hunt for scent. You're merely teaching him to stop when he sees the bird flush. Nestle the launcher in the brush so that it appears the bird is taking off on its own, and don't let the dog see you place the launcher.

When Pup approaches the launcher, either you or an assistant will launch the bird (if you have a manual launcher, an assistant is needed to pull the release cord). When the dog sees the bird flush, blow the "sit" whistle. You're teaching him to stop to flush by sitting when he sees the bird fly.

Here's the Step-By-Step Approach:

When the bird is in position, walk Pup on a thirty-five-foot check cord toward the pigeon, which is downwind. The check cord gives you control. If the bird is launched and Pup takes off running after it, you must be able to stop him with the check cord or you'll be set back in the training.

When you're approximately twenty-five feet from the bird, launch the bird. When Pup sees the bird fly, blow the whistle command for "sit." If he does not sit, blow the whistle command for "sit" again, and this time apply continuous pressure with the electronic collar. If he has been properly reinforced on the basics, he should sit immediately.

If Pup remains seated during the flush, step over and praise him. If he does not obey the "sit" command and keeps running after the bird, stop him with the check cord and blow the "sit" whistle.

Blow the whistle command "sit" as soon as Pup sees the launched bird.

Pup should be steady to the flush and shot, making the retrieve only when you release him.

After you've launched the first bird, move to another launcher, if you have one, that has previously been loaded with another bird. If you only have one bird launcher, have your assistant reload it while you hunt Pup in another area so he won't see the bird being placed. Have the assistant plant the launcher in a different part of the field, downwind of the approach you and Pup will make. Move toward it again and flush the bird. When Pup sees the bird flush, blow the whistle command for "sit." After a while, he should get the idea that he is supposed to sit when he sees the bird fly, or "stop to flush." When he is doing that, praise him and call it a day.

What if you don't have a bird launcher? You can always plant the pigeon without a launcher. It has been my experience that a pigeon will fly on its own when you're about twenty-five feet away. Pigeons, however, will also often take a notion to fly before you're ready. That can be frustrating and time-consuming.

If you can't get a bird launcher, be inventive. You could make an effective launcher from a wooden box with the lid attached to a long string that leads back to your assistant in the bushes. Simply yanking off the top of the box may not be enough to make the pigeon fly every time, though. Try removing the top with one string while jerking the box with a second string. See what works for you.

Use Your Nose

When Pup will sit on the sight of the bird flushing, it's time to let him get a scent of the bird. Here you'll be teaching Pup to scent the bird, flush it, and sit while he marks where the bird goes down.

Pointing breeds can range quite a distance from the hunter because they will freeze (point) on scent of a game bird and stand motionless until the hunter gets close enough to make a good shot, if things go as planned. But when you're upland bird hunting with a retriever breed, the dog should not be all that far out in front of you, so that you can get a shot when the bird is flushed. Happily, most retriever breeds don't range far. When the dog starts to "get birdy," as they call it, that's your signal to get over there as quickly and safely as pos-

"Getting Birdy": When scenting a bird, Pup's tail will stiffen and "spin" and he'll start to move cautiously, in a stalking mode.

sible. When a retriever scents a bird, he will "stiffen up." His tail will stiffen and start to "spin." He'll start moving cautiously, as if stalking his prey, which is exactly what he is doing. He's calling on his natural canine instincts to sneak up on supper.

Work Pup into the wind toward the bird. When he scents the bird, be ready with your launch button or have your assistant primed to pull the launch cord. When the dog pounces to flush, launch the bird. At that point he should sit. If he does not, blow the whistle "sit" command. If that doesn't work, blow the whistle com-

Once he locates the bird, Pup will pounce after it.

With the proper amount of training and field experience, you and Pup will make a winning upland team.

mand for "sit" again and apply continuous pressure with the electronic collar. The moment Pup's butt hits the ground, release the pressure.

Two points about the flush and the bird launcher. You launch the bird when you're ready at the beginning of the lesson, when the bird is downwind of you. Pup learns to sit on seeing the bird fly.

When the bird is upwind, Pup will scent the bird and he will do the flushing. You will want to launch the bird when he takes action to flush.

There are two precautions you want to take:

1. Don't launch the bird too late or Pup may catch the bird—an experience you don't want him to have. You want him to get it in his head that he needs you, his hunting partner, to down the bird. He sits and you shoot—that's the combination that gets the bird. Retrieving the dead bird is always his greatest reward.

2. Don't flush the bird in Pup's face. A spring-loaded launcher suddenly thrusting a bird in his face could frighten him. The

last thing you want to do is make the dog timid about a bird flushing. Use your own good sense. When Pup is close enough and attempting to flush, launch the bird. Don't wait until he's right on top of the bird.

The Retrieve

It's time to give the retriever something to retrieve. Place a dead pigeon in the bird launcher and hide the bird launcher in the brush. If you don't want to use a dead pigeon, use the scented dummy. You'll need your blank starter pistol for this exercise.

With the bird launcher in place, move toward the bird that is downwind of you. When Pup is an appropriate distance from the dead bird and getting birdy, launch it. He should sit on the flush and while the dead bird is still in the air, fire the blank pistol.

At this point, Pup has seen the bird "fly" and heard the shot of the pistol. He saw the bird fall and is ready to make a retrieve, but he'd better not move yet. You haven't given him permission. When it's clear that Pup is going to stay in the sit position waiting for further instruction, say his name to release him to retrieve the mark. He should then retrieve the pigeon to your hand.

When Pup is handling this part of the exercise, place a dead pigeon in a launcher that is upwind of you and the dog. Bring him toward the launcher. When he scents the pigeon and moves to flush, launch the pigeon. Pup should sit immediately. Fire the blank pistol when the dead pigeon is still in the air and wait a moment to see what your dog will do. If he is still sitting and waiting for permission to retrieve, release him to retrieve the mark on the sound of his name.

The next step is to put a live bird in the launcher. Have your loaded shotgun ready. Run Pup toward the live bird, which should be upwind. Let him scent it and move to make the flush. When he does, launch the live bird and shoot it in the air (or have an assistant do the shooting while you handle the dog). When the bird is down, give Pup permission to retrieve the bird.

The next step is to plant the pigeon, or any other game bird, in the brush without the launcher. This exercise gives Pup a chance to learn some bird sense—lessons in the ways a live bird acts in the field.

Teaching your dog to hunt upland game should give you many pleasurable days in the field. The retrievers I have seen work the uplands have great noses and make fine flushing dogs. If you can stay close enough behind them to get a shot, you should be in good shape. If Pup gets too far to your front, you can always call him in; he does not have to come all the way to you. Just call him in, command "hunt 'em up," and keep walking. He'll get the idea that you want him to work in a little closer and hunt for you. If your dog will stop to flush and retrieve the fallen bird, you and your dog can make a winning upland team.

•   •   •

ABOUT THE AUTHOR

Joseph Middleton, the co-executor of Richard A. Wolters's estate, has transformed Richard's classic Dutton books, *Water Dog, Game Dog, Family Dog,* and *Gun Dog*, into bestselling videos and DVDs, and has extended his series to *Top Dog* and *Top Dog II* in DVD and VHS. Middleton lives in North Carolina with his son, Lane, and his dog, Teddy.